THE PROBLEM WITH RABBITS

Compiled by
Pat Rees

Cover design and text illustrations
Rhian Thomas
Cover illustrations
Honor Dry

Lauren and Nibbles.

This book is dedicated to you Lauren. You and
your loving, special way with animals, will always
be remembered.

Third edition 1999. Revised from
Second edition 1998 (ISBN 0 9530317-1-3)
First edition 1997 (ISBN 0 9530317-0-5)

Available to rescues/animal welfare organizations at cost price. For details contact the publisher at the address below or telephone 0151 336 3300.

Published by Green Fork - 61, Allans Meadow, Neston L64 9SQ
Printed by J.W. Arrowsmith Ltd - Winterstoke Road,
Bristol BS3 2NT

CONTENTS

Acknowledgements

Thank you to:-

Birch Road Veterinary Practice, Oxton

D.A. Crossley   MRCVS FAVD

I.N. Holmes   BVSc MRCVS

F. Harcourt-Brown BVSc   MRCVS

The patient photographers at Rivers Studio, Birkenhead.

James Jackson of Liverpool Museum.

Freshfields Animal Rescue, Liverpool.

Mairwen Abbott, 'Cottontails' Bristol, both for her support and for sharing her expertise with me so tirelessly and willingly.

Gill Aitken for her help regarding wild rabbit re-habilitation.

Rabbit & Guinea Pig Welfare, Oxhill

Rabbit Rescue, Heswall/Hoylake.

Hillside Sanctuary, Norwich and the B.H.R.A. for their great help with circulating this book

Val Scarlett at Regency Consultants, Chester

Introduction

Rabbits are basically very inquisitive, and physically designed for an active lifestyle. They may not be super intelligent, but their inborn need to run, jump, dig, explore, and share the company of another, is exceptionally strong.

Physiologically, and in terms of bodily needs and especially instincts, there is basically no difference between wild and pet rabbits, which is why it is so cruel to keep the latter locked away in a hutch, particularly if in solitary confinement. Unfortunately, pet shops, garden centres, urban farms and even some schools, are, by example, still reinforcing and perpetuating the outdated idea that 'a rabbit belongs purely in a hutch'.

In actual fact, few people have the facilities to offer pet rabbits, guinea pigs, rats, gerbils, chinchillas etc, anywhere near a reasonably natural, humane existence, which is why at Stampers Sanctuary (from where much of the information for this booklet has been collected) we hope that in time, the idea of keeping caged pets at all, will become as progressively unacceptable as the concept of factory farming is becoming now. We would love to be able, eventually, to more or less shut our rabbit enclosures, using them only for injured or sick wild rabbits, which can be nursed and returned to the countryside.or given sanctuary for their lifetime only if there is no viable alternative.

However, the reality of the situation is that the poor old pet rabbit is still with us, and getting a very raw deal indeed within our society. Sadly, these creatures are relatively inexpensive in themselves to acquire. They are most frequently bought as a 'cheap' pet, or even a toy, without any thought to the hidden expenses of suitable caging and a humane sized exercise run.

Available pet shop hutches frequently made of thin plywood stapled together, are often leaky, have an insufficient bedroom divider, and are far too small. (There is at present no legal limit to the size of space in which you can confine a pet animal). Few shops sell runs at all, and 9½ times out of 10 in our experience, owners' good intentions to allow a rabbit to run loose all day in the garden - which of course is the best idea if it is successful - rapidly disappear when plants and lawns are decimated by eating and digging, or the rabbit is a time-consuming problem to catch at putting away time, or worse, becomes an accomplished escapologist into neighbouring gardens. Without a purpose-built run as a back up to the 'whole garden' idea, the rabbit soon becomes doomed to permanent hutching, or is at best let out just occasionally when the owner has the time or inclination to supervise, an activity which of course will be even more minimal in winter.

On the physical welfare front, these animals do not fare much better. Because parents have been conditioned over the years to consider rabbits as a cheap, easy pet (which technically they can be if you just incarcerate them in a box, like an ornament) they tend to be bought for young children, to be especially and exclusively looked after by them. The novelty soon wears off, enthusiasm for feeding and cleaning out wanes, and the rabbit is generally neglected, being out of sight and out of mind, down the garden.

Lack of supervision by parents often means irregular haphazard feeding, a dirty cage, cruel handling (by ears, etc) and an overlooking of common problems, such as overgrown teeth and nails, eye infections, ear canker, and most commonly, a soiled rear end which attracts flies, leading to maggot infestations.

Many rabbits don't really ever become sufficiently domesticated to fit into the pattern we require of them. There are, for instance, those who remain frightened by human contact, lots who, despite having daytime runs easily accessible, tend to use them only minimally, being unable to overcome their instinctive preference to be most active at dawn and dusk, the very times we have our rabbits locked away for safety. Sadly, the latter group are often diagnosed as being 'contented' in their captivity, when in actual fact they have more likely become cabbage-like, because they have lost their zest for life. (One answer is to have a hutch attached to a totally fox-proofed run to which the rabbits have access twenty four hours a day.)

Rabbits can live anything from four to fourteen years, depending on their size, breed and health, which is another reason why they become forgotten and unwanted. Teenagers generally have little time for the caged pet they acquired when they were youngsters, and many parents are begrudging about taking over pets they did not have much interest in in the first place.

The Myth of the Cuddly Bunny

Many people are misled into thinking that every rabbit bought as a pet, will automatically be the sweet and cuddly creature of story book reputation. Not so, in fact I would go as far as to say that to avoid disappointment it is best if would-be owners only go ahead with their plans, if they are happy to accept that for the main part, rabbits should be considered primarily, as what one of my rescue colleagues aptly refers to as 'spectator' pets. In other words, you must be willing to get your main pleasure from providing good, interesting, stimulating conditions for them, and watching their fascinating habits and comical antics.

Most rabbits enjoy being stroked where they stand, but if you are only interested in having a snuggly, compliant bundle for a child, or even an adult to pick up, cuddle and walk round with, don't take the chance. Only relatively few rabbits are happy to play the soft toy, large numbers of them try to avoid being picked up in the first place, are impatient when held, and often show their irritation and unease by struggling, scratching and nipping. If you are lucky enough to end up with a real softy then that's a major bonus. Sadly, countrywide, hutches are full of what are perfectly normally behaved rabbits which have failed to live up to owners 'cuddly' expectations, and so are sadly ignored.

Vicious Rabbits
Many rabbits get irritable and nippy as they go through adolescence. Neutering (both sexes) as soon as possible (see pg100) can help cut out nastiness caused by sexual frustration, but will be of limited use if the bad behaviour is genetic. Sometimes viciousness is caused by fear and you need to gradually win the rabbit's confidence with gentleness, patience and titbits. Occasionally viciousness can be attributed to the overfeeding of dried food, and not enough exercise. In a nutshell, the rabbit satisfies his hunger/energy intake in too brief a time. That can cause chemical imbalances affecting mood. The rabbit is 'fuelled up' but has no way of utilising his energy. Solution - larger, stimulating environment, and dried foods gradually cut back and replaced by slow to chew, slow to produce energy foods: hay, grass and greens.

Persistently grumpy rabbits can still be happy and entertaining as 'spectator pets', given spacious conditions, but they still need health checks, so if you can't handle a rabbit yourself he may need a more experienced home, or alternatively someone to visit and check him regularly.

Too many Rabbits, Not enough good homes

When people take on a new rabbit or rabbits, whether the source is a pet shop, garden centre or a breeder, it seems to be a common theme that they are given very sketchy information, or incorrect information about their new pet and how to keep it. Consequently you get badly cared for rabbits, massive unplanned breeding, and owners who can't cope with all the unexpected problems that rabbits can bring. It falls on sanctuaries to try and sort everything out. In 1997 more than 24,000 rabbits were taken into rescues across the country.

Breeders
Breeders are usually only interested in producing winners. Many drown or crack on the neck, babies which have no show quality. The production of new life is a miracle of nature, and to deliberately engineer births with the intention of then killing off those in the litter (sometimes all) which have committed no worse crime than not being 'show material', seems arrogant, heartless and immoral.

Equally disturbing on the other hand, some breeders in their quest for 'perfection' allow scores of baby rabbits to be born and reared in a season. Only a few will be kept, and the rest will flood the pet market. Rarely do you hear of a breeder who worries about where each and every one of these babies will end up or how they will be cared for. Already there are not enough good homes to go around, and in the gluts that occur, baby rabbits get sold for peanuts, or even given away like sweets, to live in totally unsuitable situations. I have been to shows where at the end of the day breeders have been literally brow beating the public to take unwanted stock 'off their hands' at no charge. I have seen baby animals leaving the premises in handbags, shopping bags and coat pockets.

As most breeders keep their own animals singly in small tiered cages, often in poorly lit garages or sheds, feeding only high protein dry mix and water, they are hardly going to be the ideal people to pass on advice to the public about the right way of keeping rabbits humanely, although they will doubtless be knowledgeable about illness and disease. They are however able to determine correctly the sex of the baby rabbits they breed, which is more than can be said for pet shops or garden centres.

Pet shops and garden centres

95% of the people who approach sanctuaries asking them to take in baby rabbits which their pets have produced (that they didn't expect and cannot keep or house), say that they obtained the parents from one of these two sources, and were told by the young assistants that their 'purchases' were both female. Similarly sanctuaries get requests to take one of a pair of male rabbits which have inevitably started fighting with each other on maturity. These too have frequently been sold as a 'female pair'. Inexcusably, some dealers knowingly sell a pair of males together, not pointing out that, without castration, the risk of fighting, sometimes with horrific injuries, is extremely high.

Meanwhile, all over the country, both R.S.P.C.A. centres and private rescues are overflowing with surplus, ill-treated, abandoned and 'redundant' pet rabbits. I would urge everyone who feels they do have humane facilities to offer, to by-pass breeders, pet shops and garden centres, and contact one of these sanctuaries. They can be located by visiting a local library, vets, R.S.P.C.A. branch, or by contacting animal welfare 'homing' ads in the local papers.

Only when people begin to understand and respect the real needs of rabbits, and when public attitudes frown on keeping and breeding for the show ring with all is implications, and when profit ceases to be made from dealing in 'caged' pets, will the trade decline, and the lot of the rabbit be improved.

Just waiting for a home

A pet from a sanctuary

Babies

Your local sanctuary will not always have babies available, and if you, for a particular reason, would only consider this age group, it may be necessary to obtain telephone numbers and ring around other rescues, or maybe hold on for a while until babies come in. (The same applies to particular sized rabbits like Netherland Dwarfs).

It's worth remembering that the 'cute baby' stage only lasts for about ten weeks at best from birth and, as you would not be able to take a baby from its mother until it is seven or eight weeks old, the time you can actually appreciate the 'cute stage' is minimal. 0-6 months is also the age when rabbits are at their most vulnerable from disease and fatal tummy upsets.

Many people want to start with baby rabbits because they think that they can bring them up to be tamer, gentler pets. This is to some extent a misconception. I hear of lots of people who obtain babies from shops or breeders (who breed for appearance, remember, not temperament) and these youngsters, on maturity, turn into regular Rottweilers. Rabbits rarely seem to show their true colours under a few months old, and I personally believe the temperament is controlled 90% by the genes, and only 10% by the way the animal is 'brought up'. For this reason, if a rabbit has a nice nature within him, it can be brought out at any age by regular competent handling, patient stroking and the feeding of titbits.

Many a time we have had a whole litter brought in at a few weeks old. They have all been treated the same, ie kindly and carefully, yet, when adult, some have followed one parent, who has perhaps been bad tempered, and others have inherited the other parent's placid nature.

Male or female?

The sex of a rabbit is no reliable indicator of its temperament. I have seen good and bad in both genders, and neither does the size, breed or colour play a reliable part. Overall, in my particular experience, I would say that bucks are only marginally less likely to be aggressive (unless they are neutered soon after puberty, in which case they do seem to compare a bit more favourably with similar-aged females).

There will of course always be available at sanctuaries an abundance of adult 'mongrel' rabbits. Although with a mature animal there is the possibility that the staff will be unable to tell you its exact age or medical history, at least you have the advantage of seeing its final size, and, most importantly where children are involved, you can avoid taking on animals with really vicious tendencies.

Most rescues worth their salt will ask lots of searching questions when you ring about adopting an animal. this is not obstructiveness, nosiness or officiousness, merely a way of ensuring their animals' future welfare. You have to remember that for a high percentage of rescued animals, their first experience of being 'owned' may well have included fear, pain and/or deprivation, and no way would dedicated rescue staff be willing to take chances on them being abused or neglected, even unintentionally, a second time around.

Ideally, to be fair to these animals, you need a very large diggable yet escape-proof, safe exercise space, which most people cannot provide on a permanent basis. However, being realistic, for the foreseeable future, rabbits will continue to feature as popular pets, and although obviously not able to enjoy life and indulge their instincts to the full, they can still have a reasonable quality of life in a smaller enclosure. (see page 79)

Rescue facilities
Shortage of space and unrelenting pressure of numbers, forces some rescues to keep rabbits in their own temporary care, hutched for longer periods than they would like them to be. This doesn't mean however that they are content with or would recommend their own hard-pressed facilities to be copied by adopters. There is a world of difference between an in-out rescue situation and a permanent home.

Every sanctuary and rescue I have spoken to, would love to be homing all their rabbits to 'perfect' homes, but sadly these rarely exist, so unfortunately, they have to settle for 'adequate' by compromising and setting minimum standards instead.

If, for whatever reason whether it involves danger from unruly dogs, unsuitable fencing, communal garden access, or the prohibitive cost of hutch and run - if even their minimum standard cannot be met by would-be adopters, then disappointing as it may be all round, responsible sanctuaries will tactfully point out that it would not be fair to the rabbit to choose it as a pet.

Most people who come to sanctuaries to adopt an animal are really nice, and quite understand the stance taken when the reasoning is explained to them. Often they have excellent facilities for a different sort of animal, such as a cat, but it is matter of 'horses for courses'.

Holidays

When you go away, even for a couple of days, someone armed with the phone number of your vet should be calling in each day to feed and water the rabbits, and check they are not looking ill.

Extra water bottles and slow release food dispensers are not an acceptable alternative.

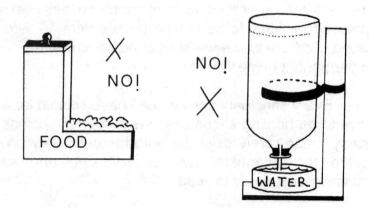

Physical Problems

Learning what every inch of your healthy pet looks like and feels like when you first get him, being familiar with his weight and watching his general behaviour, is the secret to keeping him in a healthy, happy condition. You cannot recognise detrimental changes if you are not familiar with his body and his habits, his likes and his dislikes. Never take on a pet unless you are prepared to deal with the tedious/smelly/messy problems which could arise with illness or old age.

Although children are sometimes observant, an adult must take on full responsibility for health care.

I'm not a vet so I don't attempt to advise about medical treatments but as prey animals, rabbits instinctively curb obvious displays of pain and illness, so owners need to know the subtle signs to look for and the checks to make to ensure that common health problems are spotted early, and dealt with by a vet before it's too late.

Vets can do most for an animal when they have as much information as possible, so it's helpful before a visit if the owner can spend a little time making observations so he can answer such questions as "Has the rabbit lost weight? Is he eating and drinking in his normal way - i.e. slower, more, less, not at all? Any change in his droppings or urine? Is he moving around normally? Is he still bright and interested in his surroundings, or is he quieter than usual?"

Nose
It is quite normal of course for a rabbit's nose to twitch. The speed of movement will vary considerably, being at its most rapid if the animal is overwarm or agitated, and at its slowest if he is relaxed.

Sometimes you may notice a rabbit shaking its head whilst snorting down its nostrils. This could be caused simply by dust or another irritant it has breathed in. If the nose starts to discharge white mucus, keep a close eye on whether your pet appears otherwise normal. If he is off colour, see a vet straight away. However, as long as he remains eating and running about as usual, and his breathing does not sound laboured or chesty, wait twenty four hours to see if this is a brief temporary condition which will clear on its own.

If the discharge persists after that, even if the rabbit seems well, it is probably best to get him checked out at the vet's. It is possible to miss seeing a nasal discharge in many rabbits, as they continually wipe it away, so it is necessary to routinely glance at their inside front legs to make sure the fur is clean, dry and not being used as a handkerchief!

Unfortunately, 'snuffles'. as most cold type symptoms are broadly known, can sometimes be re-occurring. Some animals can get it regularly two or three times a year. If the condition is only mild and responds well to antibiotics, the rabbit is not usually too troubled by it. We generally only have them put to sleep if they have a frequently recurring form of snuffles which is physically distressing them.

Luckily the kind of snuffles we have had so far, despite worries to the contrary, have not appeared to have been readily passed on from one rabbit to another. Some are, however, so keep a close watch on a pet's partner, and separate them if the vet feels it is a necessary precaution. (If a separation is longer than a week, be cautious with the re-introduction, it is best done outside the hutch, preferably on neutral ground).

Rabbits which are stressed out for any reason, such as being transported for more than a short time in a car, frequently have a clear nasal discharge. This is nothing to worry about.

Eyes
Eye infections are not uncommon in rabbits. These can start off looking like blobs of white pus in the inner corner of the eye. The inside of the eyelids will become red and angry, and the eye may gradually gum up and close. Ignored, the infection may get into the duct which leads from inside the lower eyelid to the nose. It may then be necessary for the vet to flush out the duct with antibiotics, sometimes several times, more unpleasant for the rabbit, and more expensive for the owner.

So - with eye infections it is very important to catch them early. The prescribed drops or ointment will then have an excellent chance of working effectively and quickly. (Don't be surprised if the vet checks your rabbits teeth when you take him in with a bad eye, sometimes pressure from a badly positioned tooth can be the cause of the problem).

Some rabbits have a tendency to 'weepy' eyes. Check for and pluck out any ingrowing eyelashes. If the 'tears' are clear, there is probably no infection. You could ask the vet if he thinks flushing the ducts to the nose would help, but if he thinks not, and the problem continues intermittently, you could, as and when necessary, try a mild ointment sold over the chemist's counter for humans, such as 'Brolene', for a few days, to see if it helps. We have had some success with it. Sometimes, there is just no curing a weepy eye, and as long as the rabbit is happy and otherwise healthy, there is usually no need to worry.

Occasionally we have had rabbits whose runny eye has caused the constantly damp fur beneath the eye to matt up and completely fall out, leaving a bald sore area. Bathing the affected area daily with plain water dilutes whatever it is in the 'tear' that causes the fur to rot. Drying the area with kitchen paper and applying a thin film of 'Vaseline' on the bald spot will control the chapping.

Where there is wetness but no baldness, it is useful to keep the fur surrounding the corner of the eye cut short to allow free flow of air and prevent fungal infection of the skin.

Another eye problem is direct injury to the eyeball, occasionally by the rabbit's own claw, but more commonly by a sharp piece of hay or straw. This looks like a fuzzy white spot or opaque area on the surface of the eyeball. It is painful and needs veterinary advice. Even with creams, the eye can take weeks and weeks to return to normal.

As a rabbit gets older, it may get cataracts. Even

younger animals may be affected if there is a genetic history of the problem. The cataracts initially look like a vague whitish patch deep down in the back of the centre of the eyeball. There is no treatment for these in rabbits under normal circumstances, and eventually the animal may go completely blind. However, as rabbits rely on their other senses far more heavily than their sight, it doesn't seem to worry them unduly, providing they can remain in the same environment. You may need to make the odd concession, like lowering its hutch if necessary to just a few inches off the floor, in case it has difficulty judging the height when jumping in. Similarly remember, after being picked up, the rabbit will have no visual bearings, so always return it to its hutch, rather than the garden or exercise pen.

Ears

Canker caused by microscopic ear mites is the most common problem with ears. A healthy ear will generally look fairly clean inside. If you hold the ear upright and peer down, there should be evident, the entrance hole to the ear canal, showing black against the pink surround.

If your pet has canker, he will probably be shaking his head from side to side a lot, trying to dislodge the cause of the irritation he feels. The entrance to the ear canal may be obscured by a brown or dark red crustiness which can smell foul. Treated early, as soon as the animal shakes his head continually, this complaint is easily dealt with by the vet. If the crustiness has not yet built up, the vet may prescribe ear drops. It is essential to complete the course right to the end, regardless of the rabbit seeming better, otherwise the most resistant mites will survive and the condition flare up again later. If the ear is not sore, the gentle massaging of the base of the ear helps the medication reach all the nooks and crannies. As inadequately treated ear problems can have serious consequences, I certainly would be hesitant to use D.I.Y. drops from pet shops. Many vets prefer to combat the mites with an injection, followed by a second two weeks later. In severe cases, injections may be the best option. The lops and cross lops we have had in seem especially prone to this problem. Many seem to have unusally narrow ear canals which easily harbour infection and infestation. Headshaking or tilting when the ear looks clean, could be caused by an infection requiring antibiotic drops. (Sometimes detectable by the ear 'clicking' with trapped pus when moved sideways).

Teeth

Maloccluded teeth, that is teeth which grow in positions which do not enable them to grind against each other to wear down, are a major problem these days. Although it can happen spontaneously, the biggest cause is thought to be dietary (see page 69) but it can also be an inherited defect. If one parent has maloccluded teeth, half the litter may develop them at some stage. It often doesn't show up until a rabbit is a year or two old, so many 'affected' animals are unwittingly bred from. Dwarfs and lops have the highest incidence rates.

As rabbits' teeth are permanently growing, if they do not wear down through grinding, they will simply grow longer and longer until the rabbit cannot eat. In the later stages of tooth problems, the animal will probably dribble and chew its own fur, but initially your pet may just have lost its enthusiasm at meal-times, so you notice a drop in the normal amount of food consumed. It may suddenly start to ignore greens or carrots, or you may notice that it doesn't graze the grass any more. Its weight may start to drop. (Box up and weigh small rabbits on top of kitchen scales. Large rabbits, weigh the difference between your own weight on the bathroom scales and your weight holding the rabbit.)

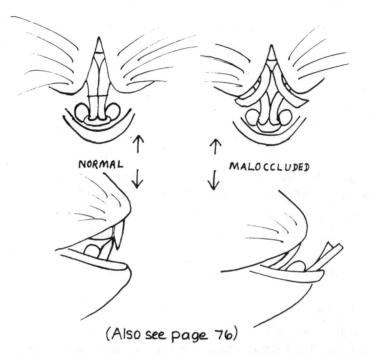

NORMAL   MALOCCLUDED

(Also see page 76)

Rabbits' teeth can become maloccluded very suddenly, over quite a short period of time, which is why it is so important to make a regular weekly check. You cannot see the back teeth, but you can easily view the front ones to look for irregularities (and possibly wetness around the lips and chin which can accompany a sore mouth).

Front Teeth

Some rabbits will stand still whilst you gently move their lips to expose the front teeth. Most will not. The easiest way is to wrap up all but the rabbit's head gently but firmly in a towel. Sit yourself on a chair and lay the rabbit on its back, along your knees, with its head furthest away from you. Gently lift the 'lips' with your thumbs and make sure the teeth top and bottom are a similar length and of straight and symmetrical appearance. If one or more of the teeth is growing at a strange angle or one is longer than the others, take the rabbit to the vet for advice. If the front teeth protrude obviously outside the mouth, owners tend to notice, but many top teeth grow backwards and upwards, piercing into the cheeks and the back of the mouth, causing dreadful pain. Without actually checking, owners cannot see this.

Awkwardly positioned teeth will need to be cut regularly by the vet every 2-5 weeks (3½ weeks on average). If the cutting is very simple and straight-forward, the vet may sometimes show an adult how to do it themselves and what to use. The main problem of DIY is the danger of accidentally cutting the rabbit's tongue or lip, or of the tooth shattering.

Latest research in rabbit dentistry suggests that although cost-wise being sometimes the only option, clipping is less than ideal, as the 'shock waves' caused by the continual cutting, apart from causing discomfort, can actually damage the attachment of the tooth and the growing tissue around the root, so grinding with a high speed drill is suggested as being preferable. Front teeth extraction is initially expensive but can be cheaper than years of 'clips'. If it is not possible for a medical reason for the rabbit to have dental attention on a regular long-term basis, it is kinder to have him put to sleep, as overgrown teeth piercing the gums or cheeks, cause painful abscesses long before the animal stops eating and dies.

Rabbits who have had their front teeth clipped cannot, because the 'bite' is altered, usually graze or eat greens or carrots in the normal way. We have found it necessary sometimes to remove the 'ribs' from cauli/cabbage leaves, and cut the remaining leaf into strips half an inch wide. Carrot can be coarse grated, bread can be diced and grass can be cut. Grooming can also present problems for the rabbit, being no longer able to tease the fur with his teeth, so watch out for sore feet and dirty bottoms.

There is a tendency, although it is by no means always the case, for rabbits with faulty front teeth, to also be suffering from back teeth malocclusion, although it frequently does not become apparent until sometimes even several years from when the front teeth are first clipped. (See page -76)

Back teeth problems

You cannot see your rabbit's molars as they are positioned far back in the jaw, so to spot problems, you have to rely on recognising the symptoms already mentioned earlier. Sometimes the back teeth can be maloccluded when the front ones are perfect (although this is less common), so if when you examine your pet, the front teeth are perfect, or they have been clipped satisfactorily, yet he still demonstrates the discussed symptoms of dental discomfort, you should suspect that his back teeth may be causing the trouble. A visit to the vet is the only solution. He may require x-rays for accurate diagnosis. If it is confirmed that the back teeth are maloccluded, you have two possibilities: having the teeth ground down under anaesthetic, or euthanasia. Each vet will have his own views on the pros and cons of this treatment, based on the successes and failures of treatment on previous 'patients'.

Malocclusion is further complicated by the fact that rabbits' teeth can grow from both ends. Dental treatment at the eating end is totally useless if the root end continues to grow, having broken through its normal 'stop' position. Such animals sadly have to be put to sleep. (We have seen a number of rabbits where the root end of a back tooth has continued to grow upwards through the jawbone into the eyeball cavity, the only obvious external symptom being drooling, continuous eye infections, and the position of the eye seeming to gradually move backwards).

Rear tooth grinding can leave the rabbit's mouth very sore, and the operation does not always enable the animal to return to normal chewing. When it does work, it is still quite likely that even if the root of the tooth is not continuing to grow, the operation will have to be repeated on the eating end in anything from 2-10 months' time. We have never been very happy overall with the outcome of back tooth grinding. It is a lot to put an animal through for an uncertain and possibly short-term result, but dental technology is improving and with the help of veterinary advice, we will continue to keep an open mind, giving consideration to having the operation performed on young otherwise healthy rabbits, if the vet feels the prognosis in the particular case is good.

Overgrown Nails

With regular exercise, most rabbits do not get overgrown nails. If, however, the rabbit has become less active with age or ill health, it may occasionally be necessary to give some or all of his nails a trim. Where the nails are white, you can see where the blood supply ends and so be confident that you are only cutting dead nail. It is not so easy on a dark nail; a good safe rule of thumb is to cut the nail back only to the same length as the fur surrounding it. This will not clip the nail quite as short as it could be clipped, but will avoid hurting your pet, and snipping a little and often is no hardship. (Where there is no fur for any reason, leave the nail half an inch long from the base).

Sore Hocks
Some rabbits get sores on their feet (usually heels), which can be very painful and difficult to heal. These can be caused by rough surfaces, oversoiled bedding, infections or inability to exercise if closely confined (a bit like bedsores). Angoras, Rex and heavyweight breeds are particularly prone.

These sores are also far more likely in rabbits which fail to groom their feet properly. Some animals simply do not seem to bother, and the feet become caked with urine, mud, excrement and anything else which then sticks. If your pet has sore feet it will probably start either staying in the hutch more than usual, or sitting in one place for long periods of time when normally it perhaps would not do so, or it may possibly be seen shuffling and lifting one or other back foot as if it cannot get comfortable sitting on them.

It is wise to check with a vet to see if there is an injury or infection, and it is probable that you may have to put straw down in the run to provide a soft surface until the foot or feet heal. Severe cases may have to be restricted to their hutch on deep straw or hay for a week or longer. 'Second Skin' available from Sports shops is recommended as useful for this condition by some sanctuaries. We haven't tried it yet, but you may like to ask your vet about its possible use in your rabbits particular case. A regular paw check is a good idea, and if you do have a rabbit which has shown a tendency to sore feet, a once-weekly soaking off of heavy mud/muck, etc by standing you pet in shallow, tepid water (only a couple of centimetres), and then drying him off well in an old towel, just before being shut in for the night, will be a good preventative measure.

Paralysis

Instant hind leg paralysis

Sometimes, for various reasons, the back legs can lose all their power, almost instantly or maybe over a day or two, and the rabbit drags itself along with one or both back legs trailing. Obviously a visit to the vet is necessary to assess the problem. We have found it worth giving the rabbit (providing it does not appear to be in discomfort, and is functioning normally otherwise) a week or two on suitable veterinary medication to see if there is going to be an improvement and possible return to normality. Some rabbits (although it is the minority) are lucky. With this course of action, great care must be taken to keep the rabbit's rear end clean, to prevent flystrike, and access to his hutch made easy. For some rabbits the vet may prescribe 'hutch rest'.

Gradual Hind Leg Paralysis

Sometimes deterioration can be over several months or even longer. (Rheumatism is often involved too). The first thing noticeable is that the rabbit just looks less 'springy' in its step when walking around. You may find that he avoids jumping into his hutch. Occasionally one side is affected more than the other and the rabbit will appear to have a lop-sided gait. (Check with the vet to see if he can prescribe anything to help, quite possible if the cause has been an injury.)

In slow, untreatable progressive cases, the legs will gradually have less and less 'spring'. Provided the rabbit is otherwise healthy, is eating, seems happy and with a bit of help is able to keep his rear end clean, it is OK to let him be, but make sure he has his hutch lowered to a level he can clamber into for food, water and shelter. With all leg weaknesses, it is sometimes necessary to chop the bedding straw or hay into short lengths, as strands tend to wrap tightly around dragging limbs, and if unnoticed, can restrict the blood supply.

As soon as the legs lose all their spring, and drag, giving the animal no support at all, it is a kindness to have him put to sleep, regardless of whether he is still otherwise happy and healthy.

'Pockets' Either Side of the Anus
Either side of the rabbit's anus, in both sexes, is a 'slit' which varies in depth from animal to animal, but resembles a closed pocket. It is quite normal for some rabbits to have dark pieces of dried natural secretions attached inside these pockets, and if there is no soreness or infection, they can be left. It is also quite normal for some rabbits to have what look like faeces filled lumps behind the skin walls of the 'pocket'.

These pockets, however, sometimes become infected, the symptom being a cream coloured cheesy discharge at the entrance to one or both slits severe enough to matt up and discolour the fur surrounding it. This complaint requires initial veterinary consultation and medication. The slits will have to be gently cleaned with a cotton bud every day by the rabbit's owner, and the prescribed cream applied. This treatment is usually rapidly effective, but needs continuing for the full length of time the vet recommends, or the infection will certainly re-occur.

Some rabbits do keep getting this problem periodically, and the only answer seems to be routine, gentle cleaning out of the slits, and keeping to hand a tube of whatever the vet advised, so that you can treat each outbreak of the problem early on. If you are for some reason unable to carry out curative and preventative care, the rabbit cannot of course be expected to endure the inevitable soreness, infections and risk of flystrike, so an alternative 'carer' will have to be found without delay. If control measures do not seem to be working out, seek veterinary advice.

Urine
The appearance of rabbit urine can vary from being a clear yellow colour to a thicker cream colour, to an almost brown colour. Sometimes it can look reddish. If the urine is heavily streaked with what could be blood, or if the whole 'puddle' looks like blood, you may need the vet. Cut out all greens and roots which may cause harmless discolouration and ensure water is easily available. Watch carefully - if the urine is still bloodlike after 48 hours, seek professional help. (Don't wait of course if the rabbit appears obviously unwell.) The colour could be symptomatic of a mild infection or may be heralding a more serious problem.

Urine Staining
Occasionally rabbits have various urinary complaint/deformities which cause them to be

permanently wet around their genitals, causing extreme soreness and smelliness, and attracting flies. If the vet says there is no infection to treat, and the problem is incurable or medically uncontrollable, the animal is best put to sleep to avoid the risk of flystrike, because rabbits urinate so often it would be almost impossible to keep them clean, dry and comfortable.

Diarrhoea
Stomach upsets can quickly become fatal in rabbits. They are best minimised in the first place by regular hygiene in the hutch and run, and by achieving a healthy balanced diet of uncontaminated foods. (Pages 69-73)

Rabbits pass two kinds of droppings - firm pellet type ones and softer ones which you may see being re-eaten directly as they are expelled from the anus. This practice, called coprophagy is normal. These droppings pass through the system a second time as part of the digestive process. Depending on the day's diet and activities, many rabbits will, however, pass fully digested droppings which vary from being dry and firm, to being far less formed, and stuck together. If the droppings become a totally unformed creamy mound, you need to judge whether your pet seems otherwise normal. If he is bright, interested, active and happy, just reduce his intake of roots and greens a little, perhaps experimenting by eliminating certain things, to see if one particular food is the culprit. (sometimes dried food - Read pages 72/73)

For some rabbits at Stampers, it seems to be normal to pass only semi-formed pellets for a high percentage of the time. Medication and temporary hay and water diets have made no difference.

If the rabbit has very runny (but not watery) diarrhoea but seems fine in himself, put him on just hay and water for three days. If there is no improvement, see the vet to check there is no problem. It seems some rabbits, like some people, pass softer faeces than others. Where there is blood or jelly-like discharge, ask the vet for advice.

The worst scenario with diarrhoea is when you open the cage or go to the run, and the rabbit is sitting huddled and very subdued in a puddle of brown liquid which may have soaked all its underside. From this stage, we have never had a satisfactory recovery. It is imperative that you get to the vet as quickly as possible for advice. Sadly, euthanasia may be the kindest option to save prolonging obvious suffering.

The overall advice with diarrhoea is - if the rabbit appears unwell with any level of diarrhoea, get to the vet fast. Never withhold water. Scorch/disinfect the hutch before a new occupant.

Abscesses

Abscesses are very common in rabbits, particularly after an injury. Ones on the main body will be detected as lumps, sometimes with a scab on top if caused by an injury. If spotted early on, these can be dealt with by the vet fairly easily and successfully either with drugs or by surgery. Unfortunately, many abscesses on rabbits occur in the head area. These can be more tricky to detect and treat. Sometimes when a rabbit is losing weight, or eats with hesitation, it can be an abscess in the throat area causing the trouble. Likewise abscesses involving the teeth and jawbone bring similar problems, and can be re-occurring. You require a vet to assess the situation.

Rabbits are basically symmetrical, so to routinely check for abscesses and tumours, stroke him simultaneously on both sides, from the very front of his nose, right back to his tail. Extend your fingers either side, under the throat, stomach and inside back legs. If one side has a swelling where the other does not, get it checked out.

Double Chin *(Dew-lap)*
Lots of rabbits get what appears to be a sagging, pouchy double chin as they get older. This 'pouch' is most noticeable in females, and can be quite large and asymmetrical in some cases. In the male it tends to be much smaller, neater and symmetrical. This pouch is natural in some builds of rabbits and needs no treatment if the animal is otherwise healthy, and not grossly overweight. Just check that the 'chin' does not feel lumpy, which may indicate a growth, and that the rabbit's skin does not get sore between the airless folds of the 'pouch'.

Strokes and Middle Ear Infections
Rabbits suffer from nervous system and brain problems, which because of the symptoms they produce, are wrongly referred to as 'strokes'. You may find your rabbit convulsing on its side, or turning around in tight circles, first one way then the other, or staggering about with its head twisted acutely to one side, sometimes with its ear touching the ground. Its eyeballs may be flicking from side to side.

Symptoms for a middle ear infection are similar to those of a 'stroke', but either way, you need the vet quickly, but without rushing and upsetting the animal. If going by car, have the rabbit in a box which is packed with hay and fairly small, so that it will not get thrown around too much. If open topped, cover the box with an old coat or towel, to darken the interior and reduce stress. If a 'stroke' is diagnosed, the vet can give an injection to lessen the likelihood of your pet having a further 'stroke' in the near future. Middle ear problems are treated with antibiotics.

Rabbits have 'strokes' and middle ear infections of varying severity, and some handle them better than others. We have found that even quite crooked heads can return to normal over the months. Some animals do not survive, of course, but those which continue to eat and get safely past the first couple of weeks, seem to go on sometimes for years without any further trouble.

Until their heads straighten, 'stroke' rabbits cannot usually jump in or out of their hutches, but after the first week, providing they are eating and seem otherwise bright, being able to walk about well, despite their crooked heads, there is no reason why they cannot go into their runs for a few hours a day, as long as there is an adult to lift them carefully.

When picked up, the twist in the rabbit's neck may become temporarily exaggerated until you put him down again. (If the worsened position persists for more than a few minutes, do not pick the rabbit up again unnecessarily for a few more days). Do everything slowly and gently. Hold the rabbit against you in such a way as to minimise the head movement, and ensure that there is food, water and shelter in the run at ground level.

If by any chance the 'stroke rabbit is being in any way harassed by its partner, the two should be separated for a while until normality returns.

Twitching
Rabbits' noses of course twitch constantly, but many rabbits have a twitch in one or other of their hind quarters. It does not appear to be indicative of a problem.

Swaying
We have noticed that quite a few rabbits we have come across over the years (mostly white rabbits or red-eyed ones) appear to lack control in keeping their heads still.

They will be looking straight ahead, and very gradually, the head sways slightly to one side or the other, as if the rabbit has dozed off with its eyes open, or lost concentration. It suddenly then seems to jolt its head back into a front facing position, and the sequence goes on repeating itself intermittently. This has never seemed to debilitate the rabbits in any way. Up to now, we have not been able to get definitive diagnosis on this behaviour. If this action accompanies headshaking, change in eating patterns or in general well-being, veterinary advice should be sought, as the swaying may be symptomatic of something else.

Sunburn
All rabbits require shade to be made available during the summer. White ones can actually get burned ears. If a rabbit's ears are obviously going very pink on top where the fur is at its thinnest and shortest, yet he continues to sit in the sun, increase the amount of shade available, especially over his favourite sitting places. If his ears look very sore, restrict his movement to 'shade only' areas for a few days.(Child friendly sunblockers/aftersun can be used). Remember, inside a wooden hutch may

seem shady, but is generally quite hot so provide other shade as well in hot weather. (See page 83)

Flystrike
Most rabbits keep their rear ends clean by grooming with their teeth, but sometimes with old rabbits, fat ones, rheumaticky ones or ones with clipped teeth, there is a build up of excrement around the anus. This is most common in animals which have always had a tendency to loose droppings. Blue bottles lay their eggs on or near the excrement. Within one to four days, depending on temperature, the eggs hatch into maggots which will either eat down through the rabbits skin, or make their way up the anus or other orifice, eating the rabbit at an alarming rate from the inside out.

This sounds, looks and is, absolutely horrific, and sadly, vets report that particularly in a good summer, this is a very common problem, which unfortunately (especially in hutchbound rabbits), people do not notice until the stage is reached when the maggots totally incapacitate the rabbit. It is inexcusable for any rabbit to be neglected like that: - check diet (page 73)

If the rabbit normally does clean its tail area thoroughly, just check once a week that it stays that way. If the tail area remains clean, there is little likelihood of 'strike' around there. With a rabbit which has a tendency to get a 'sticky' bottom now and then, it is absolutely essential, particularly in the mild to hot weather, to check its rear end at least every other day. (Cradle the rabbit firmly, on its back, in the crook of your arm, your left hand encircling its left rear leg, your right hand free to do the examination). If you do find a build up of sticky or hard excrement, you can either soak and then wash it off, or

<u>very</u> carefully, with small sharp scissors, cut the soiled fur away.

The latter method is more satisfactory if the rabbit will keep still enough for you to do it, because a less furry bottom is easier to keep clean, but the exercise does require extreme caution.

On soiled rabbits, you will need to check for the pinhead size, cigar shaped, cream coloured fly eggs: check all around the tail area before and after you start cleaning it up. The eggs are usually laid in batches, and if you find some, you can probably remove most by cutting the affected fur away. Every egg will turn into a maggot, so it is necessary to visit the vet and ask for a dusting powder such as 'Negasunt' which will kill both eggs and maggots which you may have missed.

If your pet has a permanently heavily soiled rear end, you will have to be prepared to religiously carry out the above cleaning and prevention routine every few days for the rest of your rabbit's life, or find him someone else who will. Flystrike is so horrendous that arrangements for the management of this problem (or the risk of it) cannot be ignored, delayed or dealt with half-heartedly. If you feel you are not coping sufficiently well to eliminate the possibility of 'strike' ask the vet for advice.

Flies may also lay eggs around wounds and bites, so a watchful eye should be kept on these areas too.

Wounds and bites
Except in certain areas of the body, rabbits do not tend to bleed much after sustaining even quite large bites or wounds, so if you have reason to suspect it may be

injured, perhaps following a fight with another animal, you will need to examine it systematically, parting the fur as you go. Large wounds may well need stitching at the vet's, even with lesser ones it is well worth considering going for a routine antibiotic injection to prevent all too common abscessing, which if missed can lead to a fatal infection.

Minor tears are likely to be overlooked initially because the fur is so dense, so check the rabbit again a few days after the incident, by which time you should be able to feel any damaged skin layers which will have dried and hardened around the abrasion. Dab with salt water (1 heaped teaspoon to 1 pint) for a couple of days to speed healing. If swelling occurs, see the vet. After a rabbit fight, neck and genital areas particularly should be closely checked, as these are frequently targets.

Even when rabbits are neutered, there will still be a certain amount of sexual activity, and it is common in mixed pairs for the male sometimes to pull out the fur and cause sores across his partner's shoulders. The same thing can happen to the less dominant rabbit in a 'same sex' pair. These sores are usually only very superficial, and although sometimes they take a while to heal over, because the rabbit that caused them may keep worrying the scabs, they seldom present a health problem.

Fleas

Rabbits can and do get fleas at times. They can be carried on cats, bedding, and other rabbits. The symptoms will be excessive scratching and fidgeting. You may see tiny specks of black flea dirt deep in the fur of light coloured rabbits. The fleas themselves, because of their rapid speed of movement when disturbed, may manage to stay out of sight unless the infestation is heavy. They are dark, half-pinhead sized and cigar shaped. Flea powder from the pet shop suitable for cats and kittens is generally suitable for rabbits as a standby measure, but a preparation from your surgery will have longer lasting results. Treat the hutch also.

Mites
Mites are microscopic parasites which affect the top layer of the rabbit's skin. The symptoms of mites are scaly white flakes on the skin which resemble acute human scurf. The rabbit may be scratching a lot, the skin can become inflamed and sore and the rabbit's fur frequently begins to moult heavily in affected areas, sometimes falling out in clumps.

Mites can be troublesome to totally eradicate. If it is summer, you can buy a recommended anti-parasitic shampoo from the surgery reception and bath the rabbit twice in tepid water at seven-day intervals, doing your best to really soak all the fur down to the skin, making sure you keep your pet warm afterwards until it is dry and 'aired'. You can bath rabbits in winter as long as enormous care is taken to ensure they are , after being thoroughly dried off, gradually and sensibly acclimatised to the temperature of their accommodation. Obviously this treatment can be extremely hard to carry out effectively, partly because most rabbits will not co-operate, and partly because in the shallow water of a medicated bath (rabbits would panic in anything deeper) it is incredibly difficult to get the water to penetrate the thick fur down to the skin. Powders are just as difficult to apply.

Because of all the problems of DIY mite eradication,

I wouldn't recommend it at all, it is far easier and definitely more effective to take your pet to the vet, who may decide to treat the rabbit by injection, followed by a second needle after an appropriate interval, usually about two weeks.

To help minimise re-occurrence, after each treatment for mites, it is necessary to sweep out the hutch and lightly spray the inside (or wipe with a cloth) with anti-parasitic solution, or spray recommended as safe by the vet. Allow the hutch to dry before returning the rabbit. A treatment with a blow lamp if you have one would be even more effective and save on drying time. (Young readers, please note, blow lamps are for adult use only).

Normal fur loss
Many female rabbits have false pregnancies and it is normal for them to pluck out the fur from their chests and stomach to make a nest. Some baldness may result, but it is not a problem as the fur will re-grow. Loose fur can be hung in hedges, etc, birds appreciate it for lining their nests, and in Spring particularly, can be seen collecting it.

Worms
Rabbits have their own kind of worms, but they are rarely troubled by them. The owner is unlikely to even notice them, and unless the infestation is heavy and therefore obvious, treatment is not necessary. Rabbits can be intermediate hosts for the dog tape worm, and although we have never actually had any cases of this that we have been aware of, it is another good reason for making sure your dog is regularly wormed.

Ringworm
Rabbits very occasionally contract ringworm. The

Rabbits very occasionally contract ringworm. The disease is caused by a fungus, and veterinary advice should be sought. The skin shows reddish spots, which scab, and tend to be in circular formation with complete loss of fur in the affected area. It is the same disease as in man and can be transmitted both ways.

Myxomatosis
Myxomatosis is spread by blood sucking insects such as rabbit fleas and mosquitoes. As the insect bites the rabbit, a small amount of the live virus transfers into its skin, and the animal becomes infected.

Myxomatosis is not easily spread by simple contact from one rabbit to another. If one of your rabbits is healthy and shares a hutch with an infected rabbit - providing there are no fleas present, and mosquitoes can be kept away, and given that the 'healthy' rabbit has not already been bitten by a disease carrying insect, he should stay healthy.

The incubation time for Myxomatosis varies from five to fourteen days. The first signs usually are puffy swellings around the nose and face and often the genitals, sometimes accompanied by smaller swellings on the inside of the ears. The eyes take on a 'sleepy' appearance and usually close within a day or two. More often than not, the rabbit develops a lung infection which looks like a severe cold, making his breathing very difficult. In the advanced stage he will probably be stretching his neck forward and tilting his chin upwards, mouth open, nostrils flared, trying to take in more air.

At the first sign of Myxomatosis, you need to take the rabbit to the vet. If he thinks the infection is still mild enough to 'nurse', to have the best chance, the rabbit should be kept very warm but well ventilated. Sadly, the majority of rabbits do not recover, and in some cases the vet may consider it kinder to put the animal to sleep straight away to spare it the horrible suffering that Myxomatosis can cause.

There is a vaccine available from the vet, which can greatly reduce the likelihood of Myxomatosis. This can be given to healthy rabbits over six weeks old. (From the time of injection, it takes two to three weeks to develop maximum immunity).

Ideally for the strongest protection in pet rabbits living in close proximity to wild rabbits, the vaccination is best repeated at six month intervals, but for the majority of pet rabbits, a yearly injection is sufficient. The main Myxomatosis 'season' for pets is from late summer to Christmas, so, as the protection power of a vaccine gradually diminishes with time, if you are only vaccinating once, it is best to have it done in May/June, so that the animals have the strongest protection during the worst risk times.

During outbreaks of Myxomatosis, we get some animals who remain well in themselves, but develop crusty sores on their noses, eyelids, ears and body. These scabs tend to be circular, and with time, raise up from the surrounding skin, looking a bit like lifted manhole covers. The deep scabs will eventually drop off, leaving a scar. The process can take eight weeks or more, but the animal does not usually die. The vet will advise if any ointment or dressing should be used. As long as there is no secondary infection, the scabs will still disappear even without treatment, but it may take longer.

VHD (Viral Haemorrhagic Disease)
VHD is a highly contagious viral disease affecting mainly adult rabbits - both sexes and all breeds. Unlike Myxomatosis it is mainly transmitted directly from rabbit to rabbit, although further spread via insects is considered a likely possibility.

The incubation period for this disease is only one to two days. In severe cases the rabbit dies suddenly within 12-24 hours, with no apparent symptoms.

When there are symptoms prior to death, they usually appear suddenly, are painful and distressing, and are obvious enough to send owners running for the vet, without having to list details here.

At the very end of an outbreak in an area, some animals will only contract a very mild form of the disease, and will survive to become resistant to it.

To give your rabbits the very best chance of avoiding this killer virus simply get them vaccinated each year. Ask your vet for details.

Diseases transmittable to man
Although it is uncommon, rabbits can pass on various problems to their owners such as salmonella, ringworm and other fungal infections, so it is very important to maintain a high standard of hygiene after handling animals, especially unwell ones. (Humans do not contract Myxomatosis or VHD).

Rabbit Habits

Stamping
When a rabbit is concerned or frightened he slams his back feet down on the floor to produce an amazingly loud banging noise, which in the wild is to alert other rabbits to the possibility of danger. There is little you can do about it. When rabbits go to a new home, they frequently stamp for the first few weeks, particularly at night, then settle down as they get used to the sounds and smells of their new environment.

Chinning
Rabbits have scent glands under their chins, and can often be seen rubbing their chins over all sorts of surfaces, to deposit their smell, which is a way of marking territory.

Circling
Female rabbits will occasionally run in circles round and round your feet, making little grunting noises. Nothing wrong, she's probably in season. (This behaviour also happens with females kept singly, not just with pairs). It is best to avoid letting children handle does in such an obvious mood, just in case the rabbit gets irritable and nips.

Spraying
Rabbits of both sexes will sometimes flick their rear ends and spray urine. Neutering mainly curtails this behaviour but doesn't eliminate it entirely.

Companionship

Rabbits are not naturally solitary creatures. In the wild, they live sometimes in huge colonies, sometimes in small family units, but never alone by choice. They enjoy company and get very bored and lonely when kept singly, especially during the winter, when even the most dedicated owners will be deterred from spending much time outside with their pets, simply because of the weather. Quite understandable from the owner's point of view, but not fair from the rabbit's. One answer of course is to provide company for your pet in the form of another animal.

The guinea pig (cavy) option

We are often asked about the mixing of rabbits and G.P's - Not the combination most Rescues would recommend as ideal. It <u>can</u> work given the correct environment and a placid rabbit, but sadly, many rabbits as time passes, bully their previous friend constantly, and even sadder is the fact that many owners don't realise there is a problem until the poor guinea pig is half starved, badly injured, or stressed to death. If you do go ahead, you must be permanently vigilant.

There appear to be no guarantees or absolute rules about which sexes of which species are best together. It seems to be mainly down to the temperament of the individual animals, rather than size, breed, sex or anything else, but often the most successful relationships are those made when animals have grown up together from babies, or when at least the rabbit has been very young. The only constant factor is that, if trouble breaks out, it is normally the rabbit who starts it, and the guinea pig who gets hurt, being either bitten, or suffering leg injuries during frantic chasing.

Most of the time, it is the rabbit's hormones which are to blame (caged animals do not have normal behaviour patterns, remember). In a restricted situation, male or female, it will often see a guinea pig of either sex as a potential mate, and act accordingly. The amorous advances can turn to frustration and then aggression, when the guinea pig is either indifferent or chatters his/her teeth whilst posturing with annoyance.

One important problem, even if the rabbit does not directly injure the guinea pig, is that the guinea pig may become exhausted if the harassment or chasing is constant, and suffer or even die from stress.

Hopefully, the majority of rabbit/cavy relationships will be happy, but there are a few precautions you can take if you do decide to keep these species together. It's also necessary to read up on cavy food requirements to make sure you can provide them without upsetting the rabbits diet. (For instance the cavy needs a daily supply of Vitamin C).

Better safe than sorry
Make sure you initially introduce a rabbit and guinea pig when you have plenty of time to both observe and keep checking on them. A pen on the lawn is a good place for a first meeting, as the opportunity to graze (usually irresistible to a guinea pig) will often take both animals' attention away from aggression. In weather too cold for an observer to stand about, a newspaper covered kitchen floor with a distracting pile of greens might be a possible neutral ground, or maybe an outhouse or empty garage. (If both animals are babies, trouble at the beginning is very rare, but can occasionally develop on maturity, so a watchful eye should be kept then).

Where the animals are older and one has already been living in the hutch which is to become home for both, scrub out the accommodation thoroughly with disinfectant to lessen scent triggered territorial instincts, or if the weather will not allow that, at least wipe over the interior of the hutch with safe disinfectant, so that the living territory is as neutral as possible.

It sometimes helps to lightly smear something pungent like 'Vick' or eucalyptus oil on the guinea pig's rear end fur and the top of the rabbit's nose. This helps to confuse and mask any initial smells which can sometimes trigger aggression before the animals even have a chance to get used to each other.

Hopefully, the rabbit and guinea pig will appear to get on well in the 'meeting' territory away from the hutch. (If the rabbit attacks the guinea pig from the word go, there is no point in pursuing the alliance).

If you are happy that they seem OK together after an hour or so, try them in the hutch, adding desirable titbits at the same time, and keep a close watch. Although you may feel confident about leaving the two new 'friends' in a run for the day, with access to a shelter or hutch, for safety's sake it is best to confine the animals separately for the first night.

Obviously it is easier to remove the cavy and put it inside in a cardboard box, but if the hutch was the rabbit's home and you do have the facility to remove and keep the rabbit securely for the first night, it will give the guinea pig a chance to 'put his smell' around the interior, and lay a bit of claim in the rabbit's absence. The next morning, re-introduce the pair outside of the hutch before allowing both to go back in. You will need to keep a pretty close watch for a few days.

The second precaution worth taking once your pets are sharing a home is having a small wooden escape box within the hutch, just large enough for the guinea pig to rush into, turn around, and then defend the entrance from an ill-tempered rabbit.

Hopefully, the rabbit's moments of annoyance will

be few and far between, maybe never at all, but sadly there do seem to be a fair number of rabbits who once having turned on their guinea pig continue to do so, condemning that unfortunate companion to cower terrified in a corner most of the time.

Obviously an escape box is not the answer if things have deteriorated to that stage. It is not fair to allow the guinea pig to have to spend all its life being frightened, or limited to its box, especially if it is too nervous to venture out for food and water freely.

Possible solutions

If the rabbit is fairly young, it could be worth trying neutering. It does in some cases calm them down and lessen aggression by reducing the sexual frustration. The older the rabbit is, the less likely this solution is to work, and if you see that the nastiness does not appear to be sexually motivated at all, but seems to stem from the fact that the rabbit simply does not want the guinea pig in its hutch, then separation is probably the only answer.

If things are not too bad and you are not convinced that separation is the only solution, firstly try perhaps separate food bowls, or maybe even separate hutching at night. It could be that the rabbit will happily allow the guinea pig daytime freedom of the run and hutch, and only get irritable when locked in the hutch with it at night. Even if companionship is just a few hours a day, it is better than none.

If total separation is unavoidable, please don't let the animal you remove from the original hutch be relegated to permanently living in an unsuitable box or other inferior quarters. He or she is entitled to the same well planned spacious hutch and run as your first animal. Adjoining runs will go some way to giving 'divorced' pairs a bit of company, even though they cannot safely live together.

When these two species do co-habit successfully, it is almost always essential to have a covered run. Even if your own cat is no threat, a stray could possibly come in and kill an unprotected guinea pig, although it is not unheard of for a rabbit to defend its companion, and chase the cat off.

Because in winter weather the rabbit will still want to be out and about during the day, whereas the guinea pig, disliking the cold and wet, will largely stay in the hutch, the only set up which will suit a mixed pair is to have the hutch and ramp within or attached to the run, with daytime access at will.

Another consideration when thinking of keeping rabbits and guinea pigs together is that although dwarf rabbits live from about four to six years like a guinea pig, average sized rabbits may long outlive their cavy companion and be lonely for many years, although an adult rabbit who has always been with a guinea pig is more likely to accept another one in its place.

A bereaved guinea pig, if over four years old, is best not put with a new rabbit unless you can be sure it is a gentle one who will not hassle or frighten it in its old age.

Rabbits in pairs or groups
You can of course keep various combinations of rabbits together but ONLY when environmental conditions are

right. I wouldn't recommend more than two rabbits living together for the average pet keeper because when you keep more than two animals, a pecking order starts, and it is necessary to watch out for possible bullying. (Pairs do not have to be the same size or breed to co-habit happily).

1. Two male sibling rabbits, neutered as early as possible (that is, as soon as the testicles have dropped at twelve to sixteen weeks) usually co-habit extremely happily and peacefully. You could, if facilities are large enough (at least 90 sq ft) keep three or four male siblings, but this increases the possibility of them falling out on maturity. Even two will chase occasionally and fur may fly, but other than a nip or two, there should be no serious

injury.

2.   Two non-related baby male rabbits growing up together from about six weeks and then neutered early will generally get on very well apart from the odd squabble.

3.   Female baby rabbits growing up together will co-habit happily until they are adult, but on sexual maturity, and especially if there is not a large enough hutch and exercise area, there may be a little bit of chasing round, mounting each other, pulling of fur from each other's shoulders, and mild squabbling. None of this is usually serious, but again, the more rabbits you have together, the greater the disagreement factor, and although you can often successfully keep together several baby females from different litters, if you have more than two, siblings would be advisable.

4.   Two un-neutered male rabbits, siblings or otherwise, will practically always squabble, and may even fight to the death, on maturity, especially if they suddenly smell a female rabbit's scent, perhaps wafting across garden fences or on the hands or clothes of a rabbit-owning visitor.

Occasionally I have heard of a pair of un-neutered males living happily together, but it is not, generally speaking, the 'norm'. Unfortunately, if you have two males and decide to wait and see if they do fight before you castrate, unless you are lucky and notice them having their very first disagreement and then castrate them immediately, once two males have shown serious aggression towards each other, it is frequently too late for the operation to make any difference and they will continue to fight.

5.   A trouble free permanent relationship seems to be a male from any litter with a female, when these are both acquired as similar aged youngsters. They can remain together without breeding, as long as the male is mature enough physically to be castrated by fourteen weeks old. Do not leave them together after fourteen weeks, until the male is castrated. When exact date of births are not known, or if the female is older than the male, it is sensible to keep the animals separate until the male's testicles appear, and he can be castrated, as risking a litter when so many rabbits are in rescues, is irresponsible. (Ideally spey the female as well.)

6.   If you decide to keep a mother rabbit and her son, there is always the possibility of the young buck impregnating his mother during the last critical week when you are waiting to have him castrated. Despite all your checking, testicles can drop down and appear suddenly, even overnight, and the inevitable could happen despite all your care, so to be absolutely safe, I would separate them at ten weeks, but allow them to maintain contact by adjacent runs, or if that is not possible, by having both on your knee next to each other for a stroking session for ten minutes or so a day. You should then be able to put them back together three weeks after castration, without any of the aggression problems caused by them losing the memory of each other's scent.

7.   A baby rabbit with an existing unrelated adult - some adult rabbits will accept a baby rabbit straightaway, and that is fine, but many will not. The frailty of a baby means that it cannot really be subjected to the normal chasing and banter which may occur whilst a friendship is being formed. An adult male must have been neutered for at

least a month (to allow his hormones to settle down) before you even consider adding a baby of either sex. There are two reasons for this. Firstly he will be more placid and less likely to sexually harass the youngster to death, secondly, if his new friend is female, he will not later maker her pregnant, and if it is male, he will be less motivated to attack it as it reaches maturity - at which point it will be essential to castrate the new male, to prevent future fighting. With bucks, where there is a choice, adding a baby female is preferable to a baby male. An adult female could similarly pester and stress a baby, but the sex of it is less important, although a baby male must be castrated on maturity (see previous section).

The best course of action when a baby is to live with an unrelated existing adult is:

(a)   do not attempt matching at all unless you have plenty of time to oversee the situation

(b)   obtain the baby from an animal shelter where it can go back and be cared for if the new relationship does not work out

(c)   apply the same careful precautions as described earlier with guinea pigs

(d)   have suitable standby temporary accommodation ready. A baby rabbit cannot easily be contained in a cardboard box like a guinea pig overnight, as it will jump and scrabble its way out.

An alternative is to keep the two animals living separately (yet maintaining contact through adjoining runs/hutches or handling both together under supervision each day) until the baby rabbit is big enough to protect itself. You can then introduce them more safely as semi-strangers.

Introducing strangers

Although just occasionally successful, you cannot safely introduce even castrated male rabbits to each other after 5/6 months old, and even before that age, fighting is a distinct possibility, (almost certain in a small run). However the introduction of castrated males to adult females can be tried at any age if done carefully. This is not to say the new relationship will work. It is very much a matter of temperaments, and is also affected by where the female is up to in her irregular ovulation cycle.

Bereaved rabbits are best left for a couple of weeks before trying a new partner. Very elderly/frail rabbits may be better left alone rather than being hassled by a new juvenile partner.

Because our males are all neutered to prevent litters, we have never been successful with the method of putting a female into the male's hutch which breeders would do for mating purposes. Matching neutered male to female (or female to female) requires a different approach altogether, needing time, space and patience. (Where both animals are neutered, matching is made easier).

Providing for pairs

At Stampers, we put the potential pair simultaneously into as large an area as possible. It is essential that this space is neutral territory, and preferably new ground that neither rabbit is familiar with. We have obstructions such as boxes, buckets, closed hutches, etc, every couple of feet, to break up the space.

As rabbits twisting and turning around obstacles while eyeing each other up tend to lose concentration if they have lots of new smells and sights to divert them, any chasing is less determined, and stops earlier. A hutch is not left open as it invites one rabbit to claim it, which could trigger territorial instincts.

Favourite greens are also put in the run to turn the attention from possible aggression to eating. More often than not, after initial minor chasing, smelling of the environment and eating of titbits, the rabbits are sufficiently used to each other to begin to settle down, although each will be unsure of itself and its status with being in unknown territory, and will generally act warily for a few hours.

Sometimes, however, the initial chasing culminates in vicious fighting rather than scuffling, and then it is necessary to split the pair and try the same thing again a few days later when one or both may be in a more easy going mood. Luckily, sometimes a new pair will get on together immediately. Adding a female to an existing male is easier than the other way around.

We have only ever had two rabbits which have refused all company totally, having acted like Rottweillers towards all comers, but we have frequently had to try as many as three or four different 'options' for some fussy females.

Given that the initial day of introduction has passed peacefully, each rabbit is hutched separately at night outside the neutral territory, and the process repeated each day for anything up to a week or so. When the rabbits are regularly observed sitting or lying happily next to each other in the run in the daytime, we then shut them in the hutch they are to share, just for a few minutes to see how they react. If all is well, we leave them hutched for a part of the day when someone can keep a close eye on them. Hopefully, by this stage, they will be friends, and if daytime hutching causes no problems, we then leave the animals together at night.

If we need to pair up two rabbits which have already proved to be difficult and initially aggressive, we resort to putting them in adjoining wire carriers, and taking them for a ten minute car ride. From taking rabbits on trips to the vet, we know this experience does not harm them, and rabbits in these circumstances seem to seek moral support from each other, and the edge is taken off any potential aggression, before we start the normal procedure of matching.

Some people may well be wondering, by now, if it can be so awkward getting a rabbit to accept another as a companion, why do we bother, and doesn't it indicate that perhaps they do not mind living a solitary life anyway? The answer to that is straightforward: the aggression is simply a natural deep-seated instinct for survival. Defending one's territory from strangers in the wild, is the difference between life and death and, as I said earlier, the basic instincts of wild and domestic rabbits are more or less the same.

Anyone watching established groups or pairs of rabbits together, wild or domestic, playing, rolling, sunbathing, snuggling together or mutually grooming, would be left in no doubt of the pleasure they get from company of their own kind.

Although just occasionally relationships between co-habiting rabbits can be a bit unpredictable as they become sexually mature, generally speaking, most rabbits having made friends with one another (with the exception of non-castrated adolescent males), will remain friendly for as long as they live together. Nevertheless, however happy the relationship, if an 'outsider' rabbit appears on the scene outside the 'pair's' run or hutch, it is quite likely that the established couple or group will turn on each other viciously and could inflict injuries. Things usually return to normal when the outsider is removed.

Warning
Care should be taken that children are warned not to allow a friend to bring their rabbit for a 'visit'. It could cause fighting as described above, or unwanted litters if the animals are un-neutered. Children could get badly bitten or scratched through either activity.

Rabbits appear to have short memories when it comes to friendship. If for some reason one of a pair or group of rabbits is removed from the accommodation for more than a few days for some reason, the remaining rabbit or rabbits frequently attack it on its return, particularly in 'same sex' pairs or groups, and especially if the relationships are fairly new. The answer is to separate them only when absolutely necessary in the first place, maintain some sort of contact wherever possible, and where total separation has been unavoidable, such as if one animal has been infectious, re-introduce them as strangers (see relevant section).

Night Accommodation

X
NO!

The criteria for housing your rabbit at night are: security from predators, shelter from the elements, comfortable bedding and adequate space to move around. Remember in winter particularly your pets will be shut in for the night from 5pm or so when it gets dark, until maybe 9am the next day. That is a very long sixteen hours out of twenty-four if their accommodation is cramped or otherwise unsuitable.

The majority of rabbits live outside, in homes especially built or adapted for them, and, generally speaking, the rule is - the bigger, the better. Local second-hand furniture shops often have large old sideboards which can cheaply and easily be converted. Some which are high but not overwide can have their floor space increased considerably by having a half shelf built in. The 1960's 'Long John' sideboards are particularly easy to adapt, and can be seen quite regularly in newspaper 'bargain' columns. As long as the rabbit's quarters end up waterproof, warm, spacious, safe and of course easy to clean and let your pets out from, it does not matter one bit if the hutch does not look very conventional.

Like many rescues we suggest around 8 sq ft (usually 4 ft x 2 ft x 2ft) as being the minimum night-time area required for either a single or a pair of average size rabbits. (Do not be tempted to settle for less just because the new pets, if still young, look so small, they will grow rapidly and you cannot always be sure how much). Netherland Dwarfs' hutches should not be less than 3½ ft x 21 in x 21 in).   So many people end up with average sized rabbits that they have been sold as young Netherland Dwarf crosses, that I think it is perhaps worth mentioning here that true bred Netherland Dwarfs weigh only around 2 lbs. They have tiny little ears, only an inch or two long, and squat squarish little faces. There are many 'small' rabbits being bred and passed on as dwarfs which may well mature as 'throwbacks' which grow larger than expected. We have found that when babies are produced from a 'cross', they usually grow as big as, and sometimes even slightly bigger than, the larger parent, not necessarily somewhere between the two. It should also be more widely known, that Dwarf French Lops are not what most people would consider a 'dwarf'. They are average sized rabbits, the ordinary Lops being huge. The important thing is that the rabbits end up in a hutch at least the appropriate size, so if their final size is uncertain, it is important to start with a large hutch.

When kept outside, whether a hutch is a conventional one or an adapted one, it will need a sloping felted roof, overhanging on all sides to throw off the rain, and should preferably be raised about nine inches off the ground. Too high and elderly or unwell rabbits may not be able to jump in safely from the ground (which may be necessary if the hutch is situated within their exercise area, although a ramp is always a possible addition providing that it is not too steep, slippery or narrow) and if too low, the hutch will tend to get damp, as well as being more awkward to clean out. It will also be more easily available to slugs, insects and mice, all of which are keen on rabbit food.

Hutches should never be facing the midday sun or prevailing weather, nor should they ever be kept in used garages, because of the danger from fumes.

A hutch from scratch

If you are making a rabbit hutch, remember it is as much effort making a small one as a large one, and as far as your pet is concerned, big is best. For one or two average rabbits, that means absolutely no less than 4 ft long x 22 inches or more wide.

The interior height of the hutch is important as rabbits instinctively like to sit up on their hind legs to observe and listen. Allow a height of at least 22 inches at the front, to 20 inches at the back.

METRIC EQUIVALENTS

8ft	-	240cm
6ft	-	180cm
5ft	-	150cm
4ft	-	120cm
3.5ft	-	105cm
2ft	-	60cm
22ins	-	56cm
20 ins	-	51cm
5.5 ins	-	14cm
3/8ins	-	10mm

Regarding the construction of a new hutch, the side and back walls should ideally come down outside and lower than the floor. (Many of the 'shop' built hutches eventually donated to us, which have been built up with the sides sitting directly on the base, leak badly as the rain runs down the sides and seeps underneath those walls and across the floor.)

The rabbit's new home should be made of sturdy wood suitable for outside use. Less than ½ inch thick wood, even when waterproofed, is too flimsy to be warm, and it will not withstand a fox attack, or high winds. (We have frequently heard of lightweight hutches being blown halfway across gardens in even mild storms, causing the death of the occupant from shock and/or injury.) Hardboard and chipboard soon get very damp, and disintegrate, putting your pets at risk from both illness and predators. (Foxes frequently will dismantle rotting hutches, forcing entry at the weakest point whether it be a crumbling wall or a bellying, misshapen damp floor).

If using shiplap or featherboard, it may be advisable to line the inside of the hutch with thin ply, as the protruding edges of overlapping wood seem irresistible to a chewy rabbit, who is perfectly capable of gnawing through a board in no time, and escaping. (If on the other hand you are not making a hutch, and have acquired an otherwise suitable but overly thin ply one, then it is perfectly possible to make it more substantial, by nailing or even better screwing featherboard over the outside).

All wood is expensive these days, but there are ways around this. There are many timber reclamation yards who sell perfectly adequate second hand wood at a fraction of the 'new' price, and it is also worthwhile asking around friends and relatives who may have wood cluttering up their shed or garage, and would be only too pleased to have it removed and put to good use. Remember though if wood is extremely old and painted, the paint may contain lead, and should be removed with a heat stripper.

Hutches require a snug partitioned bedroom, big enough for all occupants to lie down at the same time. (Usually about one third of the length in conventional hutches). The access hole from living area to bedroom should be about 5½ in x 5½ in and is best positioned at the back of the hutch (to minimise draughts) and starting 3-4 inches up off the floor. This ensures the hole is not blocked by thick winter bedding in the sleeping quarters, and prevents hay and sawdust from being so easily scrabbled from the bedroom into the living area - an exercise commonly practised by both sexes of rabbits.

On the inside of the hutch, across the front of the floor, some people like to use litterboards. These are simply strips of approximately 3/8 inch plywood about 2 or 3 inches high which are removable, and slot down into a channel made by nailing two small vertical batons half an inch apart on either side of the walls. These strips can be chewed to keep the rabbit's teeth trim, saving the main hutch from being attacked, and also act as retainers for bowls, bedding and even small rabbits and particularly guinea pigs which could be leaning up against the door when it is opened.

Experience has taught us that it is by far preferable to have doors shutting against the hutch frame, rather than fitting within it, as the doors then are less likely to refuse to close when wood swells or warps, or when thick strands of bedding stick out.

The wire on the front of a hutch is important. Chicken wire is no protection against a determined predator. Choose a much heavier duty squared weldmesh, and attach it every two inches with 'u' tacks on to the inside of the door frame. This effectively stops the rabbit chewing through either the wire or the frame, and makes it much harder for the wire to be mangled and removed from the outside by a dog or fox.

For door catches, bolts top and bottom of each door help prevent warping and are convenient and safe. Very young children cannot undo them easily, and neither can predators, whereas both can swiftly dislodge hooks and eyes, unlocked padlocks and swivel batons. (The latter soon loosen anyway and spin around uselessly). Where there are toddlers playing in the garden who are able to manage bolts, closed padlocks are safest for both hutch or run doors.

Hutches are best with doors hinged at the sides. Many are for some reason hinged at the top, which means balancing the door on your head whilst cleaning out, and the ones hinged across the bottom which open downwards to double as a ramp, run into difficulties when sawdust and bedding fill the crack and make it impossible to close the door easily. Steel hinges if you keep them well oiled are fine, but the extra cost of buying unrustable ones is worth it if finances permit, as you can be sure then that children do not get oil on themselves and yet you still have durable maintenance-free hinges.

The finished hutch can be painted externally with modern animal safe preservatives. (Well weathered creosote will not harm if you have obtained a second-hand older hutch, but renew with safe products). The floor of the hutch, unlikely to be chewed, can be varnished with a polyurethane product, providing the last coat is left several days to dry and 'de-fume' before putting in your rabbits. Varnishing does seem to strengthen the wood and help protect it from the ravages of urine.

To prevent the legs rotting if standing on grass or soil, leave the hutch whilst the legs are dry, standing overnight in four dishes of any penetrative wood preservative. (The safe ones are not ideal for this). Hopefully the dry legs will draw up enough chemical to give them a good long life, then, in the morning, tack small-holed chicken wire or 'clean wood around the legs to prevent chewing, making sure of course there are no sharp protrusions to cause injury. Standing the legs on tiles or slates will also help to preserve them.

In Winter, to help keep out the cold at night, a piece of thick polythene or carpet (not too closely fitting or it will cause condensation) can be tacked along the top of the wire door, and rolled up or down as required. It will need weighting down by being attached to a length of dowling or wood on its hanging end. It is essential to remember to roll this protection up in the mornings. Walking around where I live I see many rabbits carelessly left, sometimes all day, in total or near darkness.

If a hutch stands within a run, the outside bodywork as well as the legs may be nibbled by the rabbits. This is usually solvable by nailing lengths of wood approximately 2 in x 1 in around the bottom of the hutch. These can easily be replaced as necessary when they become badly chewed. Likewise, if rabbits are in a set up where they can jump up and sit on top of their hutches, they sometimes attack the felting at the corners, and batons nailed around the perimeter of the roof will stop this. (If a hutch has to be out of necessity situated near to the sides of an uncovered exercise pen and the rabbit is capable of jumping on to the roof, to prevent your pet escaping, it will then be necessary to either stretch chicken wire or fruit netting across the pen above the hutch area, or build up the height of the roof by constructing a 'mini' fence around the edges of it. Raising the hutch by putting bricks under the legs could be a solution, but be aware that without steps or a ramp old or poorly rabbits may have difficulty jumping in.

Alternative night accommodation
Occasionally people keep their pets safely at night without having a hutch at all. Rabbits can be kept on a straw bed in an unused garage or outbuilding, being transferred to their run and shelter during the day. This arrangement can be satisfactory providing that in the winter an inverted wooden box or tea chest or maybe a thick renewable cardboard box, complete with access hole and extra bedding, is placed in the outbuilding for the rabbits to snuggle into. (When they are resting it is easier for them to keep their body temperature up in a less open space).

A garden shed which has windows could be utilised in a similar manner, although few people have sheds which they do not already use for storage, and a rabbit loose in a partly used one would chew and damage things. The other major problem for both loose or hutched rabbits within a shed, is that unless they are situated in a place which never catches the sun, eg under trees or against a north wall, if someone forgets to open and peg back the door early enough in the day before the sun hits the shed, there is a major and unacceptable risk of the rabbits being cooked alive. A cloudy morning can soon change to sunny, and temperatures within such an enclosure can rise to killing levels in just half an hour. (Exactly like a dog in a hot car).

On balance I think it is far better to avoid the use of sunnily positioned sheds even in the winter because, again, winter changes to Spring quite rapidly and unexpectedly sometimes, and even a build up of spring sun in a closed shed can prove fatal.

Rabbits are relatively hardy, so for the normal levels of low temperature we get in this country, providing they have a dry enclosed sleeping area with lots of fresh bedding, they should come to no harm. If the temperatures drop abnormally low, for rabbits outside you may want to take extra precautions such as throwing an old blanket over the hutch in addition to the carpet or plastic door cover. If rabbits are unwell, or very young when an exceptionally cold snap occurs, you could transfer them to the shed, but bring them out again immediately the harsh, cold snap is over.

It is unwise, however, to bring rabbits into a warm room for the night or even just to handle them indoors for more than a few minutes and then put them back out into freezing temperatures, as dramatic sudden contrasts can be harmful to their health.

Have a hard look at hutch security!
This is a nice big strong hutch but a
fox could easily dislodge the swivel
catches being used on the doors. Bolts
would make it much safer for the rabbit.

Hutches and Foxes

The police advise that it is unreasonable and unrealistic these days to leave expensive tools, toys or other valuables, outside or in an unlocked garden shed and expect them to remain there in safety.

It is an accepted fact that human opportunists are likely to come one day and help themselves. Police have limited sympathy for property owners who fail to take suitable precautions to protect the things they value.

Sometimes I feel the same when I hear rabbit owners complaining that the fox has taken a pet for the second or third time, because in the majority of cases the death has been entirely avoidable. It's understandable that many people are usually unaware how strong foxes are, and how clever at breaking into inadequate hutches, but once a rabbit has been taken, no way should it be replaced until the accommodation has been upgraded and thoroughly fox proofed.

I do have sympathy for those who in innocent good faith have bought their hutches from pet stores, trusting that because these places claim to have specialist knowledge in animal care, the supplied hutches will provide suitable protection from foxes. After all, pet stores are perfectly aware that foxes frequent even built-up areas these days, and that rabbits are an obvious target.

Part of the blame lies with manufacturers. They could put more effort into commercially producing better hutches which actually do what they are required to do - ie protect a rabbit in all senses. However, it all comes back to the problem that rabbits are too abundant, and therefore undervalued creatures. Joinery firms are market led. They produce in many cases cheap, flimsy, unsuitable products, because that's all the pet shops they supply are prepared to pay for. The pet shops in their turn know they can sell three or four times as many hutches if the price is kept low. If the poorly housed rabbit is subsequently killed by foxes, or damp etc, its replacement is yet a further sales opportunity.

It would be nice if pet shops supported the cause of animal welfare by not selling anything that wasn't at least up to R.S.P.C.A's recommended standards for size and suitability. A well-built, well-maintained large sturdy hutch with a strong weldmesh front and bolts on all doors, will thwart most foxes. They are intelligent opportunists who can rapidly assess whether or not they can grab a quick meal with minimum effort, and if they cannot they move on.

Foxes generally visit at night and early morning, so in housing estates and similar environments, for the most part you do not have to worry during the daytime. However, in rural or semi-rural areas, rabbits' exercise pens should also be made secure. The risk of daytime foxes is not, as some people find it convenient to think, a good reason for keeping rabbits hutched permanently. If they cannot be adequately protected without denying them exercise, they should not be kept at all.

Bedding and Hygiene

For ease of cleaning, the base of the hutch should be covered either with whole newspapers, or a 3cm thickness of white wood shavings. (Red shavings, etc, are unsuitable as hardwoods are frequently treated with chemicals). Shavings are preferable for those rabbits who spend a lot of time amusing themselves by digging up the floor of their hutch and shredding paper!

Either kind of covering will probably need changing every two or three days. Some rabbits, however, are neat and constantly favour just one corner as a toilet. This is very convenient because you can just quickly scoop out the soiled patch on a daily basis, which means the whole hutch will then only have to be completely cleaned out)to avoid a build up of germs or disease) every ten days or so. It is also possible that the rabbits may use a litter tray of some sort if it is placed in the 'soiling corner' they have chosen, which could make cleaning out even easier. Some people take a little of the rabbits soiled bedding from its previous home to place in the area they want the rabbit to choose. It does seem to work sometimes.

For scraping out sawdust, a swan neck hoe or a large triangle wallpaper stripper, are the best tools for reaching into the corners.

Although not essential in warm weather, bedding straw will be required for winter. It is best to pay a little extra and get good quality barley straw, rather than buying cheap dubious bedding which may be harbouring harmful mould and excessive dust. Many people prefer to use hay as bedding, this is fine, it is actually warmer than straw in the Winter, but again it must be of good quality and, as it is dearer than straw, the cost could be prohibitive. The bedding straw or hay will of course get soiled and damp)particularly if the toilet corner happens to be in the bedroom, which frequently happens) and must be thrown out with the wet sawdust. Where hay is used as bedding in an area which does not get soiled, it will probably get eaten, and will require topping up daily.

From time to time, female rabbits, although not pregnant, will have the urge to nest build. They frequently strip all the fur from their bellies and chests, mix it with whatever is available in the way of grasses, bedding, leaves etc and arrange in the bedroom of the hutch. It is best to leave the nest where it is for a few days, cleaning under and around it if necessary, because if you take it away totally during a general clean out, it can stress the rabbit into overplucking herself whilst frantically trying to replace her nesting materials. Once she has lost interest in the nest you can discard it.

Once a year, preferably on a hot summer's day, it is a good idea to thoroughly scrub out hutches and shelters with disinfectant. Rinse with a bucket of clean water, and make sure the hutch is properly dried out before returning the rabbits. In between times a disinfected rag can be wiped over the surface of the hutch as required, followed by a rag wrung out in plain water.

The manure which is removed from the hutch and run should be composted if possible. Sometimes a neighbour is glad of it, newspapers and all, to dig into the bottom of runner bean trenches, etc. It is worth asking at the local allotment if anyone is interested - it could even lead to a regular supply of rabbit greens!

Cleaning equipment

Shovels, hoes, buckets and anything else used for cleaning out the rabbit hutch or run, should be cleaned regularly. If you have two sets of rabbits in separate accommodation, ideally each should have their own equipment to avoid spreading disease.

In between scrubbing the tools every fortnight, the easiest method of keeping them hygienically is to keep to hand a household plant sprayer full of disinfectant. Each time cleaning out is completed, the tools can be rinsed in water, then misted with the solution. Brushes require immersing weekly in disinfectant and being left to dry out. As this drying time can be lengthy, it is actually handy to have two brushes, one in use and 'one for the wash'.

Storage for bedding

If you have space for them, it is cheaper to buy bales of shavings, straw and hay. To minimise the mess from the latter, they can be stored in an old sheet sewn across the bottom and sides and tied at the top, forming a large bag. Although bin bags are handy for holding day to day amounts of loose hay or straw, compressed bales (or even half bales if you are sharing with a friend) will tend to sweat and become musty when stored in plastic.

Stolen food is always tastier!

Food

For years, rabbits have been fed concentrates (usually mixes) as the staple part of their diet. As research progresses, it is becoming more apparent that to lessen boredom and stress, and to keep his teeth and digestive system 'tip top', ideally a rabbit needs his daily energy requirements supplied at a slow steady rate, not in unnatural bursts from quickly eaten dry food. This means that like his wild relatives he actually *needs* to be chewing low energy high fibre foods like grass, hay and other green forage, for many hours a day. This in turn ensures that his ever-growing teeth wear down in the natural way, minimising malocclusion (overgrown teeth so commonly seen now). See page 76

Rabbits 'hooked' on dried food.
Rabbits are creatures of habit. Radical changes stress them. Many adults would rather starve than change to eating lots more grass/hay. A large percentage of adult rabbits on dried food will already have a degree of malocclusion which may prevent them from chewing extra fibre. Existing adult rabbits are therefore largely unsuited to a huge dietary change, but can still have their diet improved by being offered more hay and grass and ensuring that dried foods are balanced and not overfed. Future generations of rabbits should be fed much more fibre, from weaning onwards. This much, most experts agree on. What remains in dispute is whether we need to feed rabbits dried food at all.

Some vets are saying that when a 'natural' diet is provided fully and properly, dried food is simply unnecessary. Their advice, basically, is that in Summer rabbits must have good meadow hay available, and should be out grazing their own grass for at least part of every day. In Winter, as well as the hay, ideally standing grass should be given either as grazing, or pulled freshly, but as it isn't always available, a supplement of fresh domestic greens and veg will suffice as a 'stand in'.

Other vets are saying they definitely agree with promoting the grazing of grass and an increased hay intake, but are less comfortable about eliminating dry food entirely. They fear that (a) many owners will, in the long term, fail to provide adequate 'natural' diet after forsaking dried food, perhaps leaving rabbits deficient in minerals or vitamins, and (b) young rabbits themselves, for various reasons, may not actually eat enough of what *is* provided. Inexperienced owners may not recognise early enough if the 'new' diet is failing. For these reason they prefer at present to advise a very small amount of high fibre (14%+) dry food be kept as a safety net supplement to hay/grasses/roots/greens offered.

Our advice? Be honest and realistic, then choose!
IF you have total confidence in your ability to provide grass (preferably grazed), hay and a wide variety of quality fresh roots and greens every day, and you are committed to monitoring weight and progress closely, backed up by regular 'check-ups', go for the benefits of the 'natural diet'. IF you have doubts about managing to provide the natural diet 'fully and well' all the time, go for the small supplement. Perhaps the more basic question people should ask

themselves is - IF they <u>can't</u> provide the grass which research shows to be so important to a rabbit's health, is a rabbit the right pet for them to have?

Whatever diet you start a baby rabbit on, I wouldn't give them any greens except small amounts of growing grass (potted is a safe option, cut grass ferments too quickly), until they are three months old. From them on you can introduce roots and greens gradually until they are eating adult helpings by six months of age.

So that you keep regular contact each day, and he associates your visits with pleasure, try splitting your pet's greens, roots (and dried supplement if he's on one), into two 'meals' - a morning one and an evening one (useful for enticing him back into his hutch to be shut in for the night). Rabbits are creatures of habit, so choose two convenient times and try to keep to them. (When you're late, it's not unusual for a rabbit to demonstrate his feelings by throwing his bowl around with his teeth!)

Greens/forage
Most rabbits love grass, fresh green foods and roots. Where the 'natural' diet is being applied, their regular daily provision becomes essential. As has been said, fresh grass is what's best for rabbits, preferably grazed, but longer grasses can also be picked freshly,(a couple of fistfuls a day). Don't use mower clippings as fresh grass cut into tiny lengths starts fermenting immediately, causing tummy upsets. (All greenery should be from weed killer free areas unsoiled by dogs. All leftovers must be removed daily.)
For maximum enjoyment, go for lots of variety, small

amounts of each food introduced gradually. Try groundsel, dandelion, chickweed, sow thistle, clover, vetch, plantains as well as a wide range of domestic greens (not lettuce, potato or rhubarb). New growth from brambles and hawthorn hedges are also enjoyed, as well as apple and pear twigs. Consider growing 'potted' greens, e.g. dandelion to pick leaves off in Winter, and try growing carrot leaves from cut tops placed in a shallow tray of water.
Use only very fresh greens, none from the freezer, and no frost damaged ones (although rabbits nibbling frost covered plants in the garden come to no harm.)

Regarding the possibility of offering your pet a poisonous plant accidentally, rabbits have a fairly high tolerance to toxins, and providing a large amount of any one harmful plant is not its only food option, it's unlikely the rabbit will eat much of it. Buttercups are toxic, but a bit here and there in a run on the lawn will not actually hurt, although I'd remove it for young rabbits. Ragwort, yew and laburnum pods are poisonous and should definitely be removed from a rabbit's reach.

There are some domestic rabbits who don't seem to cope very well with greens without getting diarrhoea. In those genuine cases, amounts must be kept low and experiments carried out to see what they tolerate best. However, it must be said that many rabbits who have unformed droppings seemingly attributable to 'greens' are miraculously 'cured' and able to eat them happily again when dry food is temporarily eliminated, and a high intake of hay restores their gut health before returning to a much reduced level of dried food. (Not for rabbits with chewing problems, a high fibre pellet may be more suitable for them. See a vet.)

Dried foods

Dried foods, if you're using them, should never be given on a 'top-up' basis. The average rabbit who also eats some greens and hay should only have a small fistful (25g)a day. Decrease for dwarfs, increase for large breeds and weight losers. Look for modern high fibre brands (14% min. 20% ideal), perhaps a pelleted one for 'picky' eaters.

Overfeeding dry foods - problems!
1) Nutritional imbalance if it's a 'mix' as rabbits will 'fill themselves up' on just the parts of the mix they prefer. (Possible aggression, page 2.)
2) Your pet gets fat, lazy and unhealthy.
3) Rabbits feel too full to bother eating sufficient natural fibre (hay/grass) needed for slow, even energy production, digestion and trim teeth.
4) Rabbits may not re-eat the nutritious soft partly digested pellets they expel. These stick to tail fur and attract flies. (See page 25 and 30)

Hay
Rabbits should be given old fashioned meadow hay containing lots of mixed leafy grasses, presented freshly each day, in a wall mounted hay rack where it can't get soiled. The way to test for a good bale is to force your hand like a knife deep down between the 'wedges'. Scrabble your fingers and extract a handful of hay. Smell it! A sweet fresh smell indicates a worthwhile bale, a musty aroma means the bale has been compressed whilst still damp, and harmful bacteria and mould can be present which cause stomach upsets. It is also best to ask the farmer for hay which has been baled at least 2-3 months, as some experts say that 'too fresh' hay can cause digestion problems. Your chosen bale should be greenish if

possible and should not produce a cloud of dust if you give it a healthy patting. Dispose of baling twine safely to prevent entanglement by wildlife.

Dried grass

Packs of naturally dried cut grass can be obtained from pet shops and some vets. It should not be used to totally replace fresh grass, but it's invaluable for those odd times as a meal when you have failed to get 'the real thing', and in smaller quantities as a treat alongside hay to add a bit of choice and variety to your rabbit's diet. (Do ensure an adequate water supply to accompany this product.) See back page for details.

Drink

Water should always be freely available. The amount consumed will vary from animal to animal, depending on diet, age and health. Hot weather can both increase your rabbit's intake, and cause a bottle to drip itself empty, so check frequently. There's no excuse to leave a pet without. Heavy untippable bowls seem to be preferred by many rabbits, probably because it's a more natural way of taking water, and for the carer, they are quicker to both clean and fill.

Rabbits up to eight months are best having bottles, as there is then less chance of their water being contaminated by hutch debris causing tummy upsets. Watch out for faulty ones - some fail to dispense water properly so check that the air bubbles rise as the rabbit drinks, and that the water level drops, so you are confident your rabbit isn't going thirsty. In Winter the metal necks tend to freeze up solid even when the water in the bottle appears unfrozen, so check regularly for blockages. Keep bottle necks clean with pipe cleaners and bottles with bottle brushes.

In temperatures where water freezes over within minutes of you providing it, there is not a great deal you can do, except start off with warm (not hot) water, and perhaps change to a bowl so that rabbits can quickly drink a good helping. (A couple of socks lagging the bottle is recommended by some people, but it's still essential to double check the water hasn't frozen in the metal spout.) Unfrozen water must be made available in icy temperatures at least twice a day and preferably more often.

In hot weather, even if you normally use bottles, I think it's nice to also provide a bowl of water, perhaps in the run, so that your animals can have quick and easy drinks. Change water daily.

CHEWING GRASS HELPS TO PREVENT

THE HORRORS OF MALOCCLUSION

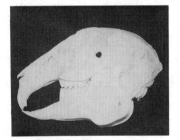

almost normal

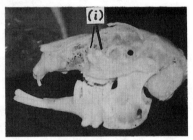

roots into the eye socket (i)
and lower jaw

spurs into
the cheek

roots into the
lower jaw

overgrown →
lower incisors

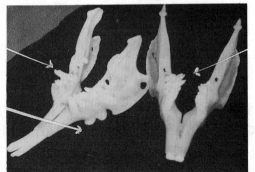

Spurs across
the tongue

normal lower
← incisors

Exercise

You only have to look at the build of a rabbit to realise that it is built for running. Those long back legs give it the power to run, twist and turn with phenomenal rapidity. Obviously, in the wild, the primary purpose for the rabbit's agility is to enable it to escape from its prey, but there is not doubt that they love to run as fast as possible, just for the fun of it on frequent occasions. I have watched both wild and domestic rabbits repeatedly take of at top speed, stop dead, do an on-the-spot jump with all four feet in the air to change direction, land and charge off again. No danger at all; just sheer exhuberance. Even the old rabbits we have here will play chasing games.

Pet or prisoner?
Most of the adult rabbits that come into the sanctuary are pathetic, redundant pets, who, like most of their kind, have been permanently hutched, sometimes for years. They have never felt the sun on their backs, the earth beneath their feet, or even the pleasure of any movement

other than a couple of miserable paces in either direction. I never cease to be amazed that relatively few people seem to have a problem with that - yet imagine the outcry if your neighbours were keeping a small dog or cat in similar conditions down the garden. Rabbits may not be as intelligent, but their instincts are equally as strong.

Many people defend their decision to restrict their rabbit to a hutch by insisting that it is quite happy where it is and it does not like being out, because once, when they put it in the middle of the garden, it just sat there looking terrified or it ran under a bush and hid. Well, of course this can happen temporarily, a permanently hutched rabbit is often institutionalised, it needs time to adapt. All I can say is that out of all the rabbits that have passed through the rescue, we have never ever had even one that has not shown absolute delight at its new found freedom, once it has had a little while to adjust. Exercise on a daily basis also makes a vital contribution to healthy bones and muscles.

Rabbits between eight weeks and six months must be allowed out for some exercise, but protected from gorging on greens and getting wet or cold however.

Providing the exercise area
Rabbits in good health, from about six months old, should have the use of as large an exercise space as possible, all and every day, the year round. Providing they have access to a partly enclosed shelter with a dry floor, to use if they want to, even frost and snow will not worry them. Some days the may sit out in the drizzle, other times they will stay in the shelter even when the weather is pleasant. It is important that they have this choice.

What area?

The absolute minimum exercise area we would re-home any of our rabbits to is about 32 sq ft (rectangular shape rather than square being better for both exercise <u>and</u> catching purposes). Really, they deserve more so that they can actually run as opposed to hopping and ambling about. Occasionally we are happy with a smaller sized permanent exercise run, where for part of the day it is possible for the rabbits to have access to a much larger space under supervision.

If the rabbits are to be offered a wired off section or the complete garden for all day use (whilst still of course having access to their hutch or a day shelter) it is important to ensure that boundary fencing is both high enough (at least 3ft 6inches) and escape proof at the bottom. Where practical, it is a good idea, if the rabbits appear to be diggers, to sink slates, bricks or wire under fencing. This gives you time to observe hole digging and fill in before any escape takes place. We have noticed that, generally speaking, the greater the exercise area, the less determined the digging.

You must be sure that in a situation where other people's dogs could come up to the outside of your fence, that the height is even greater.

Gates should be protected from being accidently left open by binmen, unexpected visitors or children, by either bolts or a spring-loaded hinge. Remember that although toddlers may not be able to reach a gate catch one year, they will certainly be able to in time.

Before agreeing to making the whole garden available, bear in mind that two rabbits can completely devastate a small garden. They will strip the bark of young trees (although plastic tree guards are available from nurseries), bite at roses and shrubs, dig up bedding plants and generally eat and damage most things with the possible exception of hydrangeas, peonies and daffodils. They may also scrabble the lawn turf. If you are a keen gardner, it is much better to allocate them a specific wired off area to chew away in. That way, they will not cause the anger and frustration that can cause people to leave them locked away in a hutch.

Where there are small children playing regularly in a garden, it is also better really, from a hygiene angle, for the rabbits to have a separate enclosure.

If rabbits do have the main garden, wherever power tools are going to be used, mowers, hedge clippers, strimmers etc, it is necessary to temporarily hutch your pets to prevent biting damage to the cables (even when the tool is not actually switched on).

Cats

When people are considering whether to roof pens or not, we often get asked whether cats will attack rabbits. Generally speaking, cats do not pose a threat except possibly to small babies or tiny Netherland Dwarfs, although they will frequently sit close by and watch them with great interest. I have never personally seen a cat attacking a rabbit (although I have seen many rabbits chasing cats) but I have in the past spoken to one or two people who have insisted that a particularly agressive tom cat has snatched their small rabbit.

Cats, however, are territorial, and you will soon notice which cat, if not your own, has 'charge' of your garden. If you watch, and this one is OK with your rabbits, you probably have little to worry about, as it will usually warn off intruding felines by spraying in strategic positions.

Framed runs
Where rabbits for whatever reason cannot be given the garden or a wired off section of it, the best alternative, especially if you need to protect them from predators, is a roofed woodframed pen a minimum of 8 ft x 4 ft. This could be built as one unit or in joined sections if extra mobility is required. Ideally it is most convenient for an owner, if the night hutch either stands within this run, or is joined to it by an access pipe or something similar. That way when the appropriate door is opened in the morning, the rabbits can let themselves out of the hutch and come and go at will, eliminating the common problem of owners getting fed up with having to physically carry rabbits morning and night to and from a separate run.

Where doors are left open all day, they should be fixed firmly open so that they cannot close in the wind, and a bowl of water provided in the run when the water bottle attached to an open door cannot be reached.

If the hutch stands outside the pen, the pen roof need only be two feet high. If the hutch is within, the height of the pen will have to accommodate it.

When planning your framed run, it is a good idea to choose the width of wire you are going to use, first. It is less wasteful to build the frame to fit the wire and sometimes a lot easier. In low roofed pens where you cnnot stand up, it is essential to have an opening roof. Most are hinged in two or three sections for convenience.

Many people build low pens without a removable roof, which requires you to either crawl through an opening section in the side, or tilt the whole pen up whilst you try and get hold of the rabbits. Neither method is convenient, and rabbits often escape during the procedure.

Rabbits in small pens on earth or grass will often dig enthusiastically. Females are the worst culprits , it is they who do the burrow digging in the wild, although males are often seen having a scrabble at the loose dug out soil, shoving it about in a half-hearted manner. The answer is to lay chicken wire across the pen floor. A small holed wire is better in a mobile run so that rabbits do not catch their feet in it, but a two inch hole is sufficient to deter in a fixed pen where the wire will soon bed down.

Particularly where rabbits' exercise runs consist solely of concrete surface, you can make life more interesting by adding a slice of tree trunk to sit on, and by providing some sort ot container, half full of soil or peat to scrabble about in. A large deep wooden seed box or an old baby bath with drainage holes drilled through would both be suitable. Lots of rabbits will play with empty plant pots, lengths of drainage pipe etc, and will enjoy chewing at and throwing around thickish lumps of tree branch.

Daytime shelter
Whatever sort of exercise area or pen your rabbits have, they must have a daytime shelter as mentioned earlier, and where hutches or shelters are within pens you have to be sure that they are positioned to provide shade in summer at all times of the day, bearing in mind of course that the sun moves. Inside a wooden hutch on a hot day, although shaded on at least the bedroom side, is not

sufficiently cool, and heat exhaustion can occur.

It is essential to provide shade within a run which has the hutch accessible, yet standing outside it. The best option is a simple flat roofed three sided box about a foot high, raised a couple of inches off the ground by the corner supports being made longer than the attached wooden sides. Being very well ventilated, this offers shade all day long either under it or at the side of it, with the added benefit of the rabbit enjoying jumping on and off it from time to time, or even using the box as a 'look out' seat.

In Winter, exercise areas should never be so low lying that they become waterlogged, and in geographical areas where snow may lie on the ground for more than a few days, an exercise area must be kept swept for the rabbits. Paving stones are useful for raising the level in parts of runs that may get muddy easily.

A final word on daily exercise runs

I have had it said to me by breeders that rabbits should be individually and permanently caged, because in that sort of sterile environment they will live longer because you have more control over hygiene and less problems from outside influences. My answer is that children kept in a tiled room with no visitors or germ-carrying toys, books, etc, would probably never get infections, injuries or colds either, but it would not be a worthwhile or kind existence. Quality of life is the all important consideration. Despite the alleged risks, most of our rabbits live long, healthy lives, but even if the breeders were partly right, I would rather have rabbits hopping and scrabbling about, sunbathing, rolling and playing together for seven years, than have a bored, frustrated, miserable prisoner for ten.

Handling

Usually, the more regular gentle handling rabbits have, the more trusting they will become. There are nevertheless quite a number of individuals who, despite all efforts to befriend them, reject human contact altogether, and scratch, growl or bite when being picked up looks imminent. However, even though they may hate actually being lifted, most rabbits will, with a little time and patience, respond to stroking and cuddling if sat on a firm surface, by keeping still and lowering their heads or backs with enjoyment. A lesser number will allow themselves to be held whilst being petted.

There are several ways to pick up rabbits, and it is best to use the one which suits both the owner and the size and temperament of their rabbit, because when wrongly held these animals can struggle so violently that they can damage their spines, in some cases causing paralysis.

"I'm not sure of the best way to get hold of him" is the phrase we hear over and over from first time rabbit owners, so although the following instructions may sound complicated on first reading, they are necessary, as followed step by step they make picking up easy for the owner and more comfortable for the rabbit. Children will need help and guidance to get it right.

After a few practices, picking up the rabbit correctly becomes automatic. The rabbit may not like it all that much, but he has to be handled to have his health checks, therefore he needs to get used to it. It's best to practise, somewhere that the rabbit can't escape from if he jumps out of inexperienced arms and I also suggest quickly crouching towards the floor if you suddenly feel the rabbit irreversibly about to leap off you, at least then he stands less chance of being injured.

1. With a very skittish, nervous animal, face it to your left and calmly stroke from nose to tail with your left hand to get it relaxed. With your thumb still stroking the ears, leave your left hand gently cupped over the rabbit's head and eyes (to prevent him shooting forwards) and simultaneously with your right hand press down gently but firmly to gather a large scruff of loose 'flesh' across its shoulders. (Too small an amount of skin will pinch the rabbit, as will gathering it from too close to the base of his ears). As soon as you have hold of the scruff, lift and turn the animal towards you, immediately moving your left hand to cradle under its bottom. Rabbits should never be lifted solely by the scruff, and should never ever have their sensitive ears held.

No! No! No!

(For more placid animals, one of the following two methods may be preferred):

2.   Face the rabbit towards you. With your left forearm firmly against the right side of the rabbit's body, bend and cup your fingers underneath its bottom. At the same time, slip the fingers of your right hand under the rabbit's chest behind the legs. Lift up and bring towards your chest, finally moving your right hand to rest firmly across the rabbit's shoulders.

3.   Face the rabbit away from you. Briefly using your left hand as a brace against the rabbit's left should, slip your right hand under the rabbit's chest, thumb pointing upwards behind the rabbit's right leg, index finger sliding between the rabbit's front legs, and the rest of your fingers behind his left leg. Move your left hand to support the rabbit's bottom, and lift. From this position, the rabbit can easily be put down elsewhere or turned to be held sideways against your chest, gently clamped in position by your right forearm. Extremely tame rabbits will allow you to ease them back to be cradled in the crook of your arm.

Once a rabbit is snuggling against you, many will feel more secure and comfortable if manoeuvred to lie across a crooked forearm, their noses tucked into your inner elbow.

When returning a rabbit to a cage after holding, it is often a good idea to put one hand over its eyes when you get to within a couple of metres of its home, because impatient or nervous animals, as soon as they see their hutch, will take a massive leap to get there, long before you are ready to put them in carefully. This can result not only in an injured rabbit that falls short of the hutch, but really deep scratches on the person who has been the launching pad!

Once you are right up to the hutch, you can either reverse picking up instruction No 2, with the rabbit being placed in backwards very exactly, or you can dip down and lean sideways into the hutch entrance, uncover the rabbit's eyes, and allow him to step off you.

When holding a rabbit against you always support it under the bottom and have a reassuring hand across its shoulders to steady it.

Breeding

I think that, if you have already read the first part of this book, you will by now be aware that at Stampers, we have very strong views about breeding from rabbits. We feel that ideally very few of them should be kept as pets at all, because most people just cannot provide the facilities these animals are really entitled to. Therefore there's no need for all the breeding that's going on.

There are already thousands of surplus and unwanted rabbits both young and old, abandoned in sanctuaries across the country. In some of those shelters, healthy rabbits which are not homed within their allocated time are having to be destroyed to make room for further unwanted ones which are brought in. There simply are not enough homes to go round, and the problem is getting rapidly worse. Breeding? - In two words, PLEASE DON'T!

Pregnant does

Occasionally people take over a stray rabbit or one from a friend or neighbour, only to find that within a couple of weeks it has built a hay and fur nest, and a few days later produced a litter (gestation is about 31-34 days).

They will be pleased to know that, in most cases, rabbits give birth to and look after their babies without problems. The owner's difficult task: start looking for good homes!

If you suspect a new doe could be pregnant because she is running around with mouthfuls of hay and plucking her fur, it is important not to upset her at this time. Increase her food rations, give extra hay and bedding and, if she is with another rabbit, move that one out temporarily. Leave the nest alone, do not try and clean out the hutch, avoid lifting her, and keep dogs, children and noisy machinery at a distance.

Discreetly peep in at the nest every morning from when it appears. When the nest is started, it is a mixture of hay, leaves, grass, moss or anything else the doe fancies using from the run, mixed witht just a bit of her fur. Two or three days or less from the birth, she will add large amounts of fur from her chest and tummy.

Care of the babies
As soon as the nest 'moves', the babies have been born. (Any number from one to twelve, but five to six is average). If it is necessary to either remove any obviously dead baby, or to replace a scattered live one in the nest, firstly give the doe some greens in the 'lounge' side of the hutch, or better still in the run. Bearing in mind pregnant or nursing does can be vicious, quietly slide an upright piece of plywood into the bedroom against the dividing wall, blocking off the access hole. Put a thin polythene bag over your hand and handle some soiled litter so that no strange smells will be put near the nest. Once you have initially sorted out dead and scattered babies, it is best to leave well alone.

If no babies have appeared after a week or so, it is likely the female is having a phantom pregnancy. This is very common and not usually a problem. Leave the nest for four or five more days and then clear away. If babies are born dead or all die soon after birth, the doe's greens should be stopped as they will promote milk production which she no longer needs. Emotionally, female rabbits show relatively little distress at the loss of a litter, but if teats become hardened or inflamed a visit to the vet is indicated.

The babies, gestated for only thirty-one days, are born blind and naked. By the tenth day, the eyes open and they have a covering of short fur. Milk will be taken from their mother for six to eight weeks, but they will also be helping themselves to solids from about three weeks. The doe appreciates being given a small but tallish box to stand on where the babies cannot pester her when she does not feel like being suckled.

After the birth, because the babies would fall out of the hutch, plus a risk from cats you cannot leave the hutch door open all the time for the doe to access her run, but she must be allowed out for a short period once or twice a day, for an exercise break.

Whilst she is suckling, the doe's greens and roots rations can be increased, as this will help her to produce milk. We prefer not to start giving baby rabbits greens until they are twelve weeks, and then only in tiny quantities, which increase as they grow up. This means that Mum has to be given hers outside the hutch. It seems a shame for the babies not to have greens, and lots of people do allow them to have a bit, with seemingly no ill effects, but young rabbits have such very delicate digestive systems that we have simply decided that it is safer to wait. (See page 94)

It is a good idea to remove Mum for a few days

before re-housing the babies, just so you can observe they are all eating and drinking properly. It also means they get used to being without Mum, whilst still in a familiar hutch.

The babies are ready to leave their mother at about six to eight weeks old. Hopefully by this time you will have made exhaustive enquiries and have good homes lined up. Babies are happier being re-homed in twos, but please make sure that the new owners know the correct sexes of their pets, and please, please impress upon them the merits of neutering as early as possible, if they take a mixed pair or two males.

Hand Rearing Orphans
Baby rabbits are fed by Mum only once a day, usually at night for about 5-10 minutes, so there is little need to even suspect abandonment just because she appears never to go near them. Recently born babies crawling away from the nest, shaking, crying, may however, need further observation. Replace in the nest. If the behaviour keeps being repeated and the babies get more distressed, you could remove Mum and try giving them lukewarm boiled sugared water to prevent dehydration. Return them to the nest, add Mum after an hour and see if they are still crying and crawling out the next morning. If so, it could be that they need fostering.

The younger/smaller the baby, the harder a successful rearing. Firstly, it's difficult to control the amount of milk entering a baby's mouth, too much at once easily ending up in the lungs; (usually confirmed by milk coming out of the nose). This causes the generally fatal Aspiration Pneumonia. Secondly, babies need real mother's milk to supply special gut bacteria which enables them to digest food properly thus minimizing diarrhoea risks. Substitutes are good but inferior.

What do you need?
For babies under 10 days extra warmth without overheating, is vital (80-85°F). Between changeable towels in a box in a warm area is fine. Milk - Cimicat; a probiotic (for good bacteria) - eg Proguard or Avipro; 1 ml syringe (for newborns); 2½ ml syringe (for over 3 weeks and feeding well). All available from Vets. Abidec multivitamin drops, useful extra from chemists. You can use syringes directly to the mouth but small teats added on the end are helpful. Some rescues prefer complete foster feeding sets - teats/sets available pet shops/vets or CATAC products 01234 360116. Mix Cimicat 1 part to 2.5 parts previously boiled water, add Probiotic and Abidec as per bottle instructions. Prepare only one day's feed at a time. Sterilize equipment in Milton at night and rinse.

How and how much?
Substitute feeds, less rich than Mum's milk, are required three times a day eg 9 am, 4 pm, 11 pm. There is no necessity to feed at night. Weak babies may need a fourth feed. (Permanent markers on ears helps to distinguish diners). Some babies can take 2/3 days to settle into a routine. Temperature just warm to touch.

Practise 'one drop' control (unless a foster bottle is used). Hold the baby semi upright/on its back in one hand (expect wriggling) and insert syringe or teat into the mouth. Dispense from syringe carefully, allowing a swallow between drops. As a guide, a normal 1-2 day old rabbit will consume about 2mls total over 3 feeds, a 5 day old about 12mls, up to about 30mls at 25 days, then decreasing towards weaning at 4½-6 weeks. Greedy feeders can have unlimited quantity, but to avoid choking, ensure they are swallowing between mouthfuls. Clean around the face with a tissue.

After feeding gently tap or stroke the genital area to stimulate urination (unnecessary after about fifth day). Droppings at early stages are yellowy and softer than adult pellets until they start solids. The latter can be introduced as hay (along with access to a waterbottle) at about two weeks. When all the babies are seen to be coping with that, you can then introduce growing grass *gradually*. On the lawn if it's warm and dry, 'potted' if it's Winter. (Cut grass ferments too quickly to give babies.) Avoid stress and sudden food changes after weaning as fatal digestive upsets are common especially at 6-10 weeks. It is unwise to give other fresh foods until 12 weeks (page 71). (If using a drymix, feed 'minutely' and read page 73.)

For emergency fostering try boiled water with a pinch of sugar, or better still evaporated milk $\frac{1}{2}/\frac{1}{2}$ with boiled water, dripped off a sterilized biro case or similar, into the baby's mouth.

Fostering
It is possible to give an orphan baby rabbit (wild or domestic) to a domestic foster mother, providing a) she hasn't already got a large litter b) the orphan is a similar age to her own young. Smear the foster baby with soiling from the new nest and place him amongst the existing litter to mingle smells for a few hours before allowing Mum to return.

(Special thanks to Mairwen Abbott at National Rabbit Aid for providing most of the detail for this hand rearing section).

Determining sex

Once rabbits are six weeks old, the sex can be determined, but unless it is something you are doing regularly, I do not think that it is as easy and straightforward as many books make out - so whenever it is possible to get a second opinion from someone with previous experience, I would take it.

To sex a young rabbit, you need to hold it on its back, and press down slightly either side of the sex organ, which will pull back the skin to reveal a slit in the case of a female and a short tube in the case of a male.

As the male matures, the penis grows in size, and by about 10-12 weeks his testicles will also start to be in evidence, which makes your decision making very much easier.

However, even vets have been known to make mistakes sexing baby rabbits, so - especially if you have sexed the rabbits yourself - to avoid breeding accidents routinely recheck the sexes of your animals at the twelve and 16 week mark.

A good photograph is worth a thousand words, so I hope the ones we've included, are helpful. These are adult rabbits and the differences between very young males and females may not be quite so distinct.

Castration

Rabbit castration, although increasing, is not yet a regularly performed operation by all vets, so ring around and choose a practice where they are confident about anaesthetising rabbits. A few will still feel there is a great risk with this species and advise against it, others who

The main features to try and identify when sexing young rabbits, are a slit in the case of a female, and a hole in the centre of a tiny tube, in the case of a male. The genitals of baby rabbits are miniscule, and less well defined than adults, so we have photographed adult animals to try and emphasize the essential differences. The adult male on the opposite page, unlike the entire male shown below, is castrated and therefore, like a baby male has no penis showing when pressure is applied to either side of the genitals. It must be stressed that all animals vary a little, so photographs should only be considered as a guide, and rechecking at ten, twelve and sixteen weeks is strongly recommended. During this time, in certain individuals the genital form can appear to swing from one sex to the other.

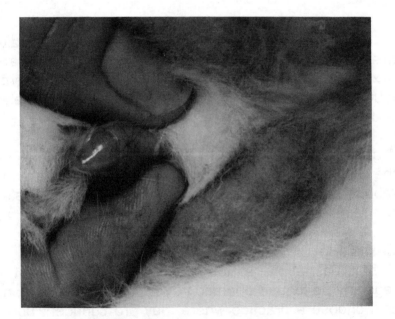

Photography by Rivers Studio, Birkenhead

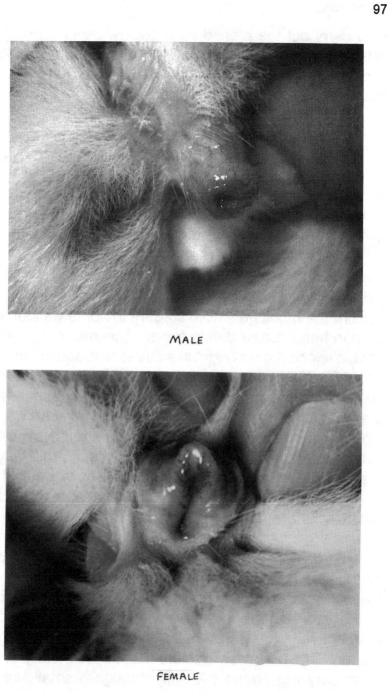

MALE

FEMALE

now carry out the procedure regularly, using state of the art, safer anaesthetics, agree that for routine surgery, there is only marginally more risk for a rabbit than a cat, providing the rabbit:

a) is in good general health and not overweight
b) hasn't been fasted pre-operatively (no need as rabbits can't vomit)
c) is given painkillers post-op (being comfortable promotes vital speedy return to normal eating)
d) is kept warm during surgery and after discharge

Aftercare
Ensure the rabbit gets from surgery to home without a big drop in temperature during transit. Summer or Winter he should spend the first night in a stress free spot indoors (at about 65-70F or 18C) At this temperature it is less 'prickly' and more hygienic for the rabbit to be sat on paper rather than hay, and easier to notice and ring for advice if the wound starts bleeding again. Food should be easily available, and warm water provided in a spill proof way, so the rabbit doesn't get damp and lose body heat. If the weather is cold, keep him in another day and acclimatise carefully before returning to the hutch.

Restrict the rabbit to the hutch for ten days, by which time the wound will be well on the mend. This is the time when the stitches are removed if the vet has not used dissolvables. Some vets operate in such a way that external stitches are not used at all. (Make sure you ask before leaving the surgery.) The buck's testicles are not removed totally, but the necessary work done internally through a small incision.

The problem to watch out for is the testicles hardening. They may be swollen the first day, but should appear shrunken after that. If one or both of the testicles remain or become swollen and hard, there may well be an infection and you need to quickly return to the vet and get things checked. (There is generally no charge for check ups/stitch removal following surgery).

When to castrate

If young males are living with adult females, to be absolutely sure of avoiding breeding accidents, they need to be separated at ten weeks old. The testicles will usually drop between twelve and sixteen weeks and then the young buck, providing he is healthy, can be castrated. On the other hand, if a young male is only with littermates, they can be left together until fourteen weeks old, but then separated until castration to be on the safe side.

A male castrated between twelve to sixteen weeks old can normally be returned immediately to a female littermate without risk of impregnation, but if he is returning to an adult female, a two week wait is necessary. With bucks castrated when they are older than sixteen weeks, more time has to be allowed - theoretically active sperm can remain in the male's body for several months after castration, but in reality three weeks seems to be a safe margin of time to wait. We have never had any 'accidents' using this time scale, although where possible I think it is prudent to be on the safe side and wait a month.

Mounting

From just a few weeks old, rabbits of both sexes will be seen mounting each other (often at the wrong end), practising mating actions. Many people think that the moment a rabbit is castrated, this behaviour will stop. Not so, in actual fact animals may carry on doing this intermittently for months. Gradually, as time passes, they decrease these activities. Two companion males may eventually cease mounting each other almost completely, but a mixed pair may still go through the motions every so often, indefinitely, particularly if the female is unspeyed. (This can sometimes result in pseudo pregnancies but we have never found these a problem.) Unneutered female pairs will always mount each other at times, neutered female pairs much less so, sometimes not at all.

Castration costs can vary unbelievably (we have heard of differences of up to 150% in the same area), so it is well worth checking around for a fair price, but only as a secondary consideration to using a confident vet.

Spaying

Spaying females has only been rarely carried out in the past, being a more complicated, risky and expensive procedure than castrating males. However, vets are now doing it more often, (mainly due to the increase in house rabbits, both sexes of which need neutering to limit spraying and facilitate house training), and there is a bonus for the rabbit because spaying gives protection from extremely common womb problems later in life. As for the females temperament, the operation may help smooth out aggression previously caused by 'P.M.T.', but will have no effect on a bad temper where the cause is genetic. The operation does however curtail a female's tendency to pester a neutered buck for sexual attention.

For pre and post operative care see page 98.

Angora Rabbits

Angora rabbits have fine wool coats of between three to five inches long, which need to be either clipped short every seven to eight weeks, or groomed daily. For that reason alone, these animals are totally unsuitable as a child's pet.

Even more of a nightmare are 'Woollies' the X breeds of the long haired rabbit world which find their way into the pet scene. Their inferior coats don't respond to even good grooming. A welfare disaster for rabbit and owner!

Personally I would like to see the Angora, and other contrived long-furred breeds, disappear altogether. Beautiful they may be, but these poor creatures do not get a good deal in life. Their heavy wool is so fine, and tats up so quickly, that even the daily grooming can be an unwelcome discomfort. They suffer dreadfully in the heat, are prone to fur balls in their stomachs, sometimes get skin problems because of the density of the fur, and often get sore feet because Angora fur wears out quickly. Clipped animals are better off, but have to regularly go through an hour or more of being held in all sorts of positions to enable the fur to be cut. It is not something they enjoy.

Both the above scenarios are situations where the Angora's coat is being dealt with - those animals are the lucky ones. I fear many of this breed just die in their hutches through sheer neglect and ignorance.

Every Angora rabbit that has arrived at the sanctuary has been in the most horrendous state. Owners have made little attempt to do anything with the rabbit's fur, many of them chose their pet because it was so cute and fluffy, but were given absolutely no indicaton by the pet shop of the grooming they would have to undertake, or the problems they could encounter.

Restricted movement
Generally, the fur on newcomers has grown to its full length, without ever being properly groomed. The ends of the fur, from roots growing inches apart, mingle together in Rastafarian style. Large fuzzy balls form, which work tighter and tighter until sometimes the poor rabbit cannot even walk without discomfort. (The worst we have had could not even walk at all). The skin beneath the matting being permanently tweeked by any movement, frequently becomes irritated and raw, and when the fur balls under the chin area become massive, sometimes the animal cannot lower its head sufficiently to eat or groom properly. In summer when bluebottle flies are abundant, any Angoras tatty and smelly around their bottoms have invariably been under attack from maggots.

Luckily, Angora rabbits do not come into sanctuaries in the same abundance as ordinary rabbits, but if you are an adult desperate to have a couple as pets and are confident that you can cope with the clipping and the grooming, please only go ahead if you can take these rabbits from a sanctuary.

Cashmere Lops

Cashmere Lops, although not as long haired as Angoras, tend to matt badly in all the awkward areas, yet the top surface of the coat frequently appears 'groomed' (see unclipped parts of neglected rabbit below) which catches people out, especially when irresponsible petshops have told them that their fluffy purchase *won't* grow into a grooming chore because 'it's a cross' or 'Cashmeres are not *really* long haired'.

Solution? To avoid matting nightmares and to discourage petshops from continuing to stock these unsuitable pets, choose 'short and smooth' - don't be tempted by that cute fluffy baby WHATEVER the sales person tells you. If you feel you are willing and able to put in the time needed to keep long haired rabbits comfortable, why not support animal welfare and take existing ones from a rescue.

Domestic to Wild?
Wild to Domestic?

People frequently ask if their redundant pet rabbit could be safely released into the wild as everything they need, grass, roots, earth to burrow in, company and exercise would seem easily available. Unfortunately it's not that simple. Coloured domestic rabbits, unable to blend into their surroundings, would obviously be at greater risk from predators, but even wild brown (agouti) coloured domestics would face other serious problems.

It is likely that although wild and domestic rabbits are physiologically and behaviourally the same, domestics, through years of selective breeding, may well have thinner coats, poorer quality vision, less acute hearing, inept burrow construction skills, and insufficient fear of predators. Even if the full fear is present, domestics are likely to be slower to react to danger. Add to all these 'minuses' the fact that a domestic rabbit having spent his life in sedentary captivity is very unlikely to be in peak fitness, he will not be familiar with his release area, he will be stressed by the massive sudden change in his environment, plus he is likely to be attacked as an intruder by other rabbits, and it soon becomes evident that your pet's release into the wild is very probably his death sentence.

There is no doubt that just a few domestic rabbits will survive as successfully as wild ones, but it should be remembered that most wild rabbits don't survive past the age of one, and to reach the age of five is very rare. Not surprising then that the release of domestic rabbits into the wild is outlawed under 'The Abandonment of Animals Act.' If you see what looks like a domestic rabbit running loose, (and you can't be sure if it's a wild brown colour) it's probably best to make a reasonable attempt to catch it. If it constantly evades you, it may well have become partly feral, so unless it's injured or in immediate danger, let it be. If it 'allows' itself to be caught relatively easily, it is either a domestic, or a wild one which is likely to be sick and requiring attention. On return to health, the temperament of a plain brown rabbit (ie whether highly agitated and panic stricken) is the best guide to judging whether it's wild or domestic.

Wild to Domestic?

Abandoned baby rabbits which require hand rearing, should be handled as little as possible (with another baby rabbit if available) and released back into the wild at six weeks old, preferably where they were found (if safe) or alternatively in countryside where other wild rabbits have been seen. They have a right to take their chances at integrating into the wild population, probably not too difficult at this age. Early evening release allows a little time to explore and familiarise before darkness and foxes come.

Injured wild rabbits too (any age) should be handled minimally. If treatment has been lengthy, a 'soft release' method of freedom is recommended. This is basically a halfway house idea where the rabbit is kept in a safe, sheltered, large penned area with food supplied, and then released after a settling period to 'escape and return' at will until he is ready to move on completely into new territory. Because this method requires a large garden or paddock backing on to suitable release land, it will probably be necessary to contact an animal rescue who will be able to suggest contacts equipped to help.

When injured wild rabbits are left with serious disabilities, their best option is to be found a neutered mate (domestic is fine), and a permanent large, safe area such as a walled garden home. (Wild rabbits should never be kept in an average 'pet' set up.) If the compromised rabbit is still agitated and unhappy in his semi-captivity, it is kinder to have him euthanazed.

Considering House Rabbits?

I wouldn't like long term, to encourage the idea of keeping rabbits as pets at all (for reasons I've already justified earlier in this book), but whilst they are still a popular choice, the more information around about the 'pros' and 'cons' of different humane housing methods, the better.

Many people these days have heard of the imported American idea of keeping a pet rabbit loose in the house, in much the same way as a cat or dog, but be warned, despite its obvious attraction, it's not a system that will be suited to most households. When an obliging easily trained rabbit with the right temperament is in the totally right dedicated household, then possibly all will be well, and the rabbit is likely to enjoy far more attention, mental stimulation and consideration than the average one living outside. The owners too can get more enjoyment because they can watch their pet from the comfort of their chair, and really get to know him (or her).

However, actually bringing an animal into your home as a permanent resident, is not a move to be taken lightly. To treat your house rabbit fairly, will definitely mean making some adjustments and sacrifices in your home, and involves commitments which must last for his lifetime. Because it is such an important and tying decision I make no apology for including such a big section on all the points that need thinking about before you go ahead. After all, if you don't know what to expect on the negative side, how can you get a balanced view to base your decision on?

Outside facilities
There seem to be differing professional opinions as to whether rabbits need a certain amount of natural sunlight to ensure their maximum health. Regardless of who is right or wrong, I believe that every rabbit has a birth right to experience its share of fresh air, outside sounds and smells, the wind in its fur and the sun on its back, so if you haven't got a suitable outside area that a house rabbit could sometimes use, then personally I feel it wouldn't really be fair to keep one. A bit like having a dog and never taking it out.

Caging in the house
Most people opt for a 'home cage' as a base for the rabbit to both rest in when he's tired of exercising, and to return to when he wants to wee or poo. You obviously must have a rabbit home big enough, so are you really prepared to have a large wood or metal cage permanently stuck in your room? Will it get in the way, take up too much space or spoil the look of your decor? It could be there for years and years. How about the inconvenience of scattered litter, stray bits of hay and fur from heavy moults?

Exercise
It's not fair to have a rabbit in the house unless you are prepared to offer him lots of free running/roaming' time. A house rabbit does not just mean keeping a rabbit caged in the house to save the owner having to go outside. Once the rabbit is relatively well house-trained, 'lots' of roaming time throughout the day and evening should add up to hours rather than minutes, otherwise, as with rabbits hutched permanently outside, you merely have a

frustrated prisoner.

Someone at home
Is there somebody at home often enough? If you are nearly always out, there's not much point getting a house rabbit at all, he'll just be lonely. If you're out a lot but not often enough to discount house rabbits completely, two would provide company for each other. This could mean double problems though. If you couldn't cope, it's kinder to leave it altogether rather than keep a lonely animal.

Patience
Are you prepared to put in the time for the initial training? Have you the patience, because success doesn't come overnight. There will be lots of toilet accidents at first (rabbit wee can stain), a one step forward two steps back hiccup as he goes through puberty, and even when he's trained there will always be the odd wet mistakes, and certainly always some stray pellets which may go unoticed and get trodden into the carpet.

Chewing

Rabbits are natures greatest chewers, so despite all

discouragement and training, its quite likely that at least now and then, and quite possibly more frequently, your house guest will attempt some or all of the following activities.

Nibble skirting board to a scalloped finish, strip wallpaper, gnaw and restyle any available wooden furniture, bite and/or scrabble any soft furnishings and generally look through his teeth at anything else which interests him - books, toys, shoes - nothing is sacred.

Most favourite items for the chop are telephone wires and electric cables. You can of course try to encase wires in plastic tubing but that's a bit inflexible and unsightly if you have more than the odd one or two and if you miss covering an inch or so you can guarantee the rabbit will find the exposed bit, and what about that jumble of TV cables? You could of course try moving and blocking off everything vulnerable as best you can everytime your pet is loose, but are you really prepared for all that inconvenience and will you still feel so tolerant in all the years to come?

Dogs/children

Is it actually going to be practical to have a rabbit loose in your particular house, or will the poor thing gradually end up shut in its cage all the time? Will children playing and darting about fall over the rabbit causing injury to it or themselves? Will doors constantly be left open allowing the rabbit to escape or access rooms you haven't rabbit proofed? How about the dog - can you trust it never to turn on the rabbit? Personally I don't think it's fair to keep what are after all natural predater and prey together; the rabbit probably won't ever feel really relaxed even if he appears to be unafraid, because he'll instinctively be aware that there's a risk and that he has no place to escape to in the confines of a room.

Neutering
Both sexes of house rabbits need neutering at about five months, earlier if you have a pair. It more or less stops the spraying of urine habit, it aids toilet training as it lessens the rabbits 'need' to leave pellets all over the place as territory markers (which even toilet trained rabbits may start to do again at puberty) and it might make for a more placid animal in some circumstances. Neutering is expensive, have you budgeted for it?

Lifetime commitment
Rabbits although averaging 7-9 years can live to be 10-14. Are you really prepared to take on a rabbit in your home for that long? Can you tolerate the fact that as a rabbit gets older, the smell of urine gets stronger and may well linger slightly in the room despite all your regular cleaning out? What about the days he may have a slightly 'off' tummy and soft, unpleasant smelling droppings?

Living in your house means your pet becomes highly socialised, dependant on the high level of activity and company it encounters. It would be mental cruelty to later banish it to live in isolation down the garden, just because its indoor requirements became a tedious inconvenience. Far better to say no to a house rabbit in the first place.

If a serious change of circumstances beyond your control means that you just can't have the rabbit living indoors any more, he should be provided with outside facilities as described in earlier chapters, and if possible, a rabbit companion. A supreme effort must be made to still give the rabbit as much of your own company as you can outside, and to bring him in whenever possible. (Without subjecting him to dramatic contrasts in temperature).

Hey!Ive finished grazing
I want to come in!

Having a House Rabbit

You've decided to have a house rabbit, so how is it all done?

The first three steps
1.   Provide a large 'home cage' and decide on its permanent position (not next to the TV or speakers nor in a draught or by radiators). Equip it with a heavyweight food bowl in a corner near the door, a water bottle, a hayrack, a branch to chew and a litter tray filled with wood based cat litter. (Clay based products should be avoided as they can cause stomach upsets in rabbits). Some people abandon their plastic litter tray in favour of a similar shaped heavy oven dish to avoid the problem of the rabbit using his teeth to tip it up. If you can get hold of a handful of soiled bedding from his previous home to add to the new litter, that will certainly be an encouragement for the rabbit to choose the right place as his toilet.

2.   Plan the rabbit proofing of the room or rooms the rabbit will be allowed to use when he's allowed out in a few days time. Until he's reasonably well trained, the room will have to stay permanently protected unless you have the saintly patience to move or alter everything that's necessary, and then put it back half a dozen times a day.

3.   Obtain your pet(s) from a sanctuary, for all the reasons mentioned in earlier chapters. Adult rabbits are no harder, and sometimes considerably easier to train,

than young ones. As mentioned before, personality and nature can change around puberty.

Ready to start
Put your new pet in the cage with enough water,   food and hay to last until the next day. Simply leave him alone for a few hours. Houses can be noisy places with lots of strange sounds and smells to become used to. The rabbit needs to be allowed to concentrate on taking in his new surroundings, without the added worry of seeing a human he doesn't know advancing towards him.

At first he'll probably sit up tall and look around, pricking his ears intently, analysing every sound for possible danger. He may stamp a bit with nervousness, then when he feels a bit more relaxed he will proceed to examine every feature of his cage. It's important not to disturb him, you want him to learn that his cage is his castle, the place he goes to rest, to eat, to be safe, to avoid attention when he doesn't want it and to wee and poo.

Bribery
After a few hours you can go quietly up to the cage and start talking to him. If he stays determinedly at the other side, just talk softly a while longer and then leave him to it for a couple more hours before trying again. If he shows interest and comes up to the wire, slowly offer a titbiit taken from a rustling paperbag, towards him whilst saying his name. If he moves away, just quietly drop it through the wire and stand back repeating the procedure at intervals.

It won't be long before your rabbit will come eagerly to the side of the cage anticipating the special titbit.

Rabbits respond brilliantly to bribery as long as the offering is desirable enough. It's probably worth trying out a whole range of things to see what he likes best. Bits of biscuit, peanuts, sultanas, a dice of carrot, celery leaf, dandelion leaf, morsel of brown bread, parsley - they all have their favourites, remember though, it's only supposed to be a taster, one quick, tiny chew. Sometimes just the noise associated with food is enougt to bring a rabbit running. Our treats are kept in a crackly cellophane bag. One rustle commands full attention. Keep practising his bribery response because you'll need it to get him back to his cage in the future.

By the end of day 2 you may need to just top up his hayrack (which you placed by the door so that he won't get disturbed too much), but don't clean his cage out, the mess won't hurt for a day or two more, and it's vital you don't invade his castle too soon. You can quickly clean it out in a few days time whilst he's out of his cage eating a carrot or something to distract him.

About day three, it's time to give him a taste of freedom, but only if he wants it. You can't reach in and lift him out because you're teaching him that this is the place he needs to be if he doesn't want to be pestered or picked up (and most rabbits arn't keen on being lifted). Just wait until he's curious and brave enough to come out on his own. (He'll probably look about six inches longer than usual as he moves forward with his front half but only slowly allows his back half to catch up, in case he decides he's made a wrong decision!).

Keep it short
Allow him about 10 or 15 minutes before saying 'home' and gently 'herding' him back into the cage, where you will

have left his titbit. Rustle the paper or make what ever his bribe noise is whilst he eats it. When rabbits want to wee, they raise their tails slightly and push or shuffle their bottoms backwards a fraction. If your rabbit shows these signs before the 15 minutes is up, slap your leg, say 'home' in a firm voice and shepherd him back to his cage as quickly as possible. The chances are high that he will rush back there anyway, because you'll have startled him.

Make sure there is a titbit in there. He'll probably eat the treat and then continue his wee in the correct place. If you actually see him poo, you do the same thing, but luckily, lots of rabbits prefer to poo in their cages whilst relaxing and eating. Its pointless reacting to his poos if you don't catch him at it. All this has to be practised many times. Some pets catch on quickly, others take longer.

If all goes well, eventually, when you say 'home' your rabbit will run eagerly back for his treat and he'll have perfected the habit of going to the cage to use his 'toilet' where he has learned he can wee in peace.

Chewing trouble

When your rabbit chews something he shouldn't or scrabbles the corner of the carpet for instance, say 'no' firmly and walk towards him. Stop moving the minute he leaves his target alone. If he simply won't stop, pretend to go to pick him up, that threat in itself usually makes the rabbit move. If he returns to the target, repeat 'no', and again move in if you have to. Most rabbits learn quickly that if they don't respond to 'no' there is this annoying threat of a human picking them up, when all they want is the freedom to mooch about and explore.

You can leave a few things around to try and otherwise occupy him such as a syrup tin filled with noisy dry beans, yoghurt pots, a ball. Some rabbits enjoy 'toys', some don't.

Gradually you will be able to leave your rabbit out for longer and longer periods without him soiling, and hopefully without him chewing things, but what about his contact with you? It's essential that fussing and stroking only takes place when the rabbit actually wants it, so he must be the one to come to you. The best way is to always have a titbit handy and just offer it if he comes near. Never try and pick him up at this stage unless he's looking unwell. You won't be doing that until all the training is over and the ground rules well established on both sides.

Eventually, with luck and patience you will end up with a confident rabbit who will come when you call (for the titbit) return to his cage on the command 'home' (for the titbit) and who may follow you round happily or lie by your side for company, because he trusts that he's the one that will always make the first move towards any interaction with you. Some lucky owners end up with a pet that will sit beside them for hours to be stroked, even jumping up onto a settee to be beside their 'person', and often licking them affectionately like a dog. Yes, keeping a rabbit in the house can have mutual benefits, but only when all the conditions are right, and there are definitely no guarantees.

NATIONAL RABBIT AID
(incorporating Cottontails Rescue)
(Reg Ch. 1064753)

The escalating numbers of rabbits being left unwanted across the country (16,000+ revealing only the tip of the iceberg in their first National Survey (1995), has led to the formalisation of the charitable organisation National Rabbit Aid. (1997 figures are 24,000+)

- Promoting good rabbit husbandry
- Providing advice and care sheets
- Discouraging breeding
- Informing and educating the public
- Listing national rabbit shelters
- Providing a telephone helpline
- Encouraging communication between rescuers

N.R.A., Bristol HQ, 7 Lilac Court, Keynsham, Bristol, BS31 2RR (Enquiries with SAE please) Tel: 0117 986 6806

****

The British Houserabbit
association P.O. BOX 346
Newcastle upon Tyne
NE99 1FA

The B.H.R.A. is a club for all rabbit lovers.
Members receive a quarterly journal 'Rabbiting On'
as well as enjoying social events and unlimited rabbit advice.
Please send A5 S.A.E. for free leaflet and membership details
****

INDEX

The Rabbit Charity

Reg Charity: 1068622
Produces "The Rabbit Habit" for its members and
'"Rabbit Healthcare" for veterinary use.
Enquiries with SAE to: PO Box 23698, London, N8 0WS

SPILLERS

Spillers produce a range of rabbit feeds which contain high levels of fibre, essential for maintaining a healthy gut. All feeds are locust bean free and contain an extra tasty pellet with all the essential vitamins and minerals your rabbit needs.

Also contained within the range is Spillers Readigrass. This is dried natural grass - all the goodness left in, only the water taken out.

Spillers Helpline: 01908 226626